Teaching Students to Learn
A Student-Centred Approach

Teaching Students to Learn

A Student-Centred Approach

GRAHAM GIBBS

Open University Press
Milton Keynes : Philadelphia

Open University Press
Celtic Court
22 Ballmoor
Buckingham MK18 1XW
and
1900 Frost Road, Suite 101,
Bristol, PA 19007, USA

First Published 1981

Reprinted 1985, 1986, 1989, 1991, 1995

British Library Cataloguing in Publication Data

Gibbs, Graham
  Teaching students to learn.
  1. Study, Method of
  I. Title
  378.1 '7'02814   LB2395

  ISBN 0-335-10043-0 (cloth)
  ISBN 0-335-10033-3 (paper)

Printed in Great Britain by J. W. Arrowsmith Ltd., Bristol

Contents

Preface

Students new to higher education, and even those new to sixth forms, are asked to tackle learning tasks which make demands on them different from any they have ever faced before. It is not simply the sheer quantity of material to be learned, or even the new responsibilities students have to take for the way they go about this learning, which makes the heaviest demands. The meaning of learning itself changes. Students have to become independent not only in their self-discipline and self-organization in order to cope with studying, but also, ultimately, in their epistemological stance.

While I passed 'A' level history at school by memorizing the eight causes of the French Revolution, history students at the institution where I now work are asked to evaluate alternative theoretical frameworks for making sense of such social changes as those associated with the French Revolution — and this in their first term, perhaps only four months after taking their 'A' levels! This sort of difference in the nature of learning tasks can be enormously difficult for students to recognize and adjust to. While teachers can help in the teaching methods they use and in making their teaching goals explicit and clear, this is often not enough. Students need time and space to examine not just the subject matter of their learning, its *content*, but also the *process* of their learning itself. Most teachers do not have a lot of experience of helping students to examine the process of their learning, and they not unnaturally turn to books on the subject for advice. However, until very recently there were simply *no* books written for teachers on this subject. There are over a hundred *How to Study* guides written for students, with advice on how to take notes, how to concentrate, and so on, but these are of very limited use to teachers. It is the ineffectiveness of simply giving advice to students that led to the development of the methods described in this book. If you feel your own students could be going about their learning in a more thoughtful and purposeful way, and you would like to do something about this in a way that does not make heavy demands on your own time or expertise, then this book is for you.

It is based on an earlier booklet: *Learning to Study – A Guide to Running Group Sessions* (Gibbs, 1977). This booklet was initially written for Open University tutors and was intended to provide them with 'off-the-shelf' exercises which they could run with their students at tutorials. Very quickly requests for copies started coming in from outside the Open University. Without publicity or marketing, I had received over 3,000 requests from all over the world by 1980, and the exercises in the booklet were being used from Japan to Brazil, and from New Zealand to Finland. There is obviously a huge unmet demand from teachers for help with 'study skills' which goes beyond the conventional giving of advice to students. This book is designed to help meet this demand by expanding and improving the earlier booklet. Perhaps most importantly this volume contains a more complete rationale. Initially I felt that the approach I had adopted to teaching students to learn was intuitively correct and seemed to work. Now I have been able to relate the approach to important developments in research into student learning. I also now have the benefit of an overwhelming amount of feedback, from others who have adopted this approach, about how it works in practice. As a consequence I feel that I now understand what I have been doing rather better than I did. I hope this understanding comes through.

The second major development from the earlier booklet is that questionnaire feedback indicated that many teachers were using the general principles embodied in the booklet, but not using the particular exercises the booklet contained. In this volume, I have emphasized rather less the exercises I recommend, and paid more attention to how to design your own exercises within the same overall framework.

I should like to acknowledge the role of Andy Northedge, of the Open University, in the creation of many of the most important ideas in this book. Andy has played a large part in the development of my thinking and I could not have written this book without him. It would have been a better book if he had been able to contribute more directly as he had originally hoped to do.

I should also like to acknowledge the help of the students who have worked through exercises with me and so helped me to improve them, and the many many people who have written to me with useful comments gleaned from the experience of trying these exercises out with their own students. And finally I should like to thank Cathy Urwin for reading the manuscript and seeing, through its inconsistencies of argument and style, ways of making it readable.

How to use this book

I have divided this book into two parts: the first is concerned with practical issues of how to actually go about teaching students to learn and the second is concerned with theoretical issues and the rationale for the teaching methods described in Part 1.

If you are in a hurry, if you need an idea for an exercise for the class you are taking in fifteen minutes time, then you are in luck. Any of the six exercises in Chapter 2 can be picked up and used without any special skills or knowledge. Choose your topic, read the Notes which go with the topic and follow the Instructions. You may also need to copy a handout for your students. These six exercises all work reliably and are very safe and easy to run. I believe this is the quickest and most effective way of finding out what this book is recommending. Off you go!

Chapter 1 addresses practical questions about how best to use these six exercises. Who are they for? When is the best time to use them? If you have the time to plan your use of the exercises, or feel hesitant about trying anything without knowing a good deal more about it, then I suggest you have a brief look at one or two exercises and then read Chapter 1.

Almost everyone who tries using one of these exercises goes on to try another. Once you are at this stage you may well want to know more about the approach I have adopted and why the exercises are in the form they are. The rationale for this approach is elaborated in Part 2 of the book. The rationale consists of discussion of four main questions: 'Why not just *tell* students how to learn?' 'In what ways do students develop as learners?' 'How can students' development be facilitated?' and 'Why use structured group exercises?' each of which has a chapter devoted to it. I have put this rationale at the back of the book because while it is important to me (and important to those who like a sound rational basis for what they are doing) it seems not to be necessary for many. People seem to be able to pick up enough rationale *experientially* by running exercises and seeing what goes on and what outcomes emerge.

Once people become committed to using the approach described in this book, they very often go on to use the general principles of the approach while abandoning the narrow confines of the specific exercises suggested here. They design exercises of their own which address learning issues specific to their students on the course or discipline within which they teach. Going beyond what these exercises offer seems to be an important part of using the approach, and so I have included a chapter specifically on designing your own exercises, Chapter 3. Unless you feel very confident very quickly, I suggest you try using one or more of the exercises in Chapter 2, more or less as they stand, *before* you go on to design new exercises for yourself. Each of the exercises has been chosen to embody a different device which can be used in its design. For example the exercise called 'Reading: using books' uses the device of getting students to do something they might not normally do in order to introduce some new ideas about using books. You may find it useful to use such devices as a part of exercises that have been tried and tested before you take them out and use them in your own way.

PART 1

A student-centred approach
in practice

How to use the exercises

This chapter answers most of the practical questions which teachers ask about the use of the exercises in Chapter 2.

Who are these exercises designed for?

These exercises were originally designed for first-year university students. Since then they have been successfully used with polytechnic students, college students, sixth-formers in schools, experienced teachers undertaking postgraduate studies, adults preparing to study with the Open University, and with mature overseas students about to start postgraduate study. Students who are already studying and have begun to encounter the realities of study seem most likely to benefit — indeed some of the exercises are based on students' experience of studying.

Most teachers seem to use these exercises with their own classes of students — in other words groups of students of similar experience, studying the same subject. However, many have run interdisciplinary exercises attended by groups of widely differing experience. It has been found to be common for third-year undergraduates and first-year postgraduates to regularly attend sessions put on primarily for first-year undergraduates. Similarly groups containing, for example, a mixture of engineers, social scientists, business studies and design students have worked regularly together. The mixture of experience, level and discipline adds to the variability of ideas and study methods and experiences, which can be very illuminating and eye-opening. It can also make it very difficult for students to transfer the rather generalized lessons learnt from the exercises to their own specific learning context. Homogeneous groups can work around study materials (e.g. essays, books) lifted straight out of their own course, which makes the whole exercise more immediate and relevant. However, this too can bring problems. Students can easily get wrapped up in understanding the subject matter, the *content* of the learning, and lose sight of the *process* of learning it. There may also be too little variability in approach and perspective to generate the controversy which can be so important in these exercises.

Over time I have probably moved away from running exercises for mixed groups towards running exercises for a group of students who know each other and are studying the same material. The advantages for group dynamics of the structure of the exercises offered here has therefore become less crucial, and the materials offered as subject matter less likely to be appropriate. I would adopt a degree of structure to the sessions, and choose my materials to suit the type of group I was to work with.

How many students are these exercises for?

The structure of these sessions enables *very* large groups of students to be handled. I have run such exercises with 450! Probably an optimum size, if ideas are to be freely exchanged and some development and *synthesis* is to take place, is twelve to forty. Above forty the structure must be followed rather rigidly as it is difficult to get useful feedback in order to respond to the group's requirements. Also the plenary stage becomes difficult to run and less productive. Groups of much below twelve become less alive. There seems to be a 'critical mass' for the generation of energy and excitement. There are fewer ideas to share and compare, and the structure becomes increasingly unnecessary until with fewer than six students it can become rather artificial and stultifying. Some of the exercises can still work well with only a couple of students, though inevitably your role as a tutor will necessarily become much more prominent and this may inhibit students considerably — some of the student-centred purpose of the exercise may be lost.

Students often have no experience of working in groups with little or no input from a tutor and some find this rather difficult. I suspect that some students may be unhappy about taking part in an exercise for more than about twenty people because they get so little 'personal attention'. Some such students may not easily come to trust their own learning and I would expect such students not to turn up after the first exercise or two unless this issue is explicitly picked up and discussed.

How long do these exercises last?

The exercises are designed to take an hour. Questionnaire feedback suggests that none of these exercises *consistently* require more or less time. In fact as many teachers find particular exercises to require more as to require less time. Some individual teachers have reported that *every* exercise required less than an hour and we suspect this to have been due to the particular style of the teacher or lack of interest of the particular students. In my own experience the time required depends on the degree to which the initial task *engages* the students in a real way and taps their thoughts and feelings about their studying. The nature and relevance of the materials used and the description of the task by the teacher seem crucial to this. Irrelevant materials presented with vague task instructions tend not to engage the students and the exercise will not last as long. I have often found an hour and a half a more realistic target if I am not to rush my students, though it seems best, if it is possible, to respond to what the group appears to need on each specific occasion rather than stick rigidly to a preconceived plan. It is sometimes hard to predict how much students are likely to discover in a task and the timing offered with each exercise can only be a general guideline.

When, and in which order, should the exercises be run?

I am *not* suggesting that you run through all these exercises in the order offered here, or even that you run through them all at all. Where teachers report having done this it seems that their students have eventually felt that the structure has become repetitive and that in any case most of the important issues had been raised and discussed after the first few exercises.

Having said that, the first exercise: 'How do we learn?' is useful as an opener. It gets the group established, well used to the approach and focuses on familiar and threat-free subject matter which students generally share with gusto and feeling. It also establishes a powerful precedent both for the value of personal experience and the differences between students. *Everyone* has bad learning experiences to relate, (even if everyone cannot always recall a good learning experience) and this makes the session reliable and easy to run. After that it may be best to respond to whatever concerns your students. It is difficult to run a good session on essay writing until your students are actually having to write an essay (or even their second essay!) and students may not perceive the importance of organizing their time until they have deadlines to meet or have even missed a deadline. Similarly it may not be sufficient that your students are attending lectures for it to be worth while running a session on taking notes from lectures. Until notes are *needed* for some other task (such as writing an essay or report, tackling a problem or preparing for a test) then note taking can become a somewhat abstract or trivially technical topic for discussion.

If you are running exercises with students whom you yourself teach then you will be in a good position to judge when the exercises will be appropriate. The exercise 'Learning from discussion' benefits from students' experience of tutorials or seminars. At the same time it is clear from much of our questionnaire feedback that it can dramatically affect the way future tutorials go, and has been used as a device by teachers to improve the effectiveness of their own small group teaching. So not too early, not too late, seems to be the rule.

I hope it is clear from these points that I would not be strongly in favour of paying a great deal of attention to students studying during, for example, their induction week. I have attempted to teach students about learning out of the context of any actual learning, and I have been chastened by the experience. If you wish to *prepare* students, then these exercises are likely to be useful only if the students are actually studying their subject during their preparation so that they have some real study experience to relate to, and work on. It is not just that content-free studying makes little sense; in addition the harsh realities and pressures of actual studying demand *compromised* and *pragmatic* rather than *idealized* solutions, and also provide the desire, or even the necessity to implement them.

Exercises on examinations tend to be left until late in the course, even until immediately before the examinations. However, most of the crucial outcomes of an exercise on revision could affect the way studying might be undertaken throughout the year. Your decision whether or not to run an exercise on revision at the *start* of the year may well depend on whether you feel that if students concentrate on the demands of the examination it will detract from their concentrating on the demands of your course!

What extra materials do I need?

With the exception of the exercise on using books, materials have been provided for every exercise. You can simply photocopy and distribute the materials as they stand. They have all been used many times both by myself and by others. However it can be very helpful to provide your students with materials drawn from their own courses: an essay to mark written by a student the previous year; an article to read

6

drawn from the references given in your last lecture; last year's examination paper; and so on. The reality of the exercises and the ease with which students can generalize from the lessons learnt to their everyday studying may be crucially influenced by the nature of the materials used in the exercises.

In addition, some examples of materials may work much better than others. One pair of essays to compare for the exercise 'The author's intention' may raise many crucial issues in an engaging way, while another pair may be dealt with and dismissed by students in a cursory way without anything important arising. As you experiment with these exercises you will probably collect materials that you have found to be potentially stimulating. Finding suitable materials can be the most time-consuming part of preparation for these exercises. I have offered some advice on choosing materials along with the instructions for each exercise.

What sort of room do I need?

Informal rooms with furniture that can be moved around are best. Lecture theatres with banked seating pose real problems and any layout that inhibits participants from facing and talking with each other in pairs and small groups should be avoided. Layouts which place heavy emphasis on an orientation towards the teacher, blackboard, lecturer or whatever authority normally dominates the room should also be avoided. It is hard enough for students to express and trust their own views without loading the dice in the favour of authority.

I usually lay the tables and chairs out so that people naturally form small groups without awkward shuffling and regrouping at each stage of exercises, although very obvious groupings of chairs in fours can also be inhibiting and make participants feel manipulated.

Despite the wrong sort of room and furniture it is still perfectly possible to run these exercises provided the conventional function of the room (e.g., as a lecture theatre) is deliberately avoided. A long introduction from a podium to serried rows of seats will estabish a passive roll for participants, whereas a quick and casual introduction from the side may avoid this. Many students have trouble adjusting to a non-passive role, especially in large groups, and architecture and furniture layout can contribute to their difficulties.

Other general advice

In addition to my own experience I have had questionnaire feedback from about two hundred teachers who have used these exercises, and a mass of correspondence from teachers all over the world who have tried the approach or adapted it to their own needs. I have been sent handbooks and course outlines that teachers have written, developed from their experience of using the approach. I also have some limited questionnaire feedback from students and quite a few accounts by students of their experiences on courses made up of these exercises. Probably well over two thousand teachers will have been using this approach, or derivations from it, in 1981, and this has generated a great deal of discussion and innovation. As a result I have a fairly accurate idea of teachers' experiences with this approach and can guess what your experience with it is likely to be.

On the positive side, these sessions seem pretty reliable: students get involved and believe they benefit; the sessions are easy to run; and tutors do not give them up after trying them only once. They seem to improve the general atmosphere, and willingness to share responsibility for learning, within the group. They save tutors planning time, and give valuable feedback on what aspects of teaching, counselling and learning need more attention.

On the negative side, students get bored with the *structure* of the sessions after a while. The rigidity of the structure can be relaxed or abandoned once the group is working well. Also, unless the purpose and general philosophy of the approach and structure of the initial sessions is explained, students can resent its 'game' element and wish for more direct advice. Some rather passive students may ask 'What do we know now that we didn't know already?' at the end of the session. It can be hard to recognize what has been gained when there is no authority behind conclusions other than one's own and one's colleagues' experiences. Some teachers have found that students welcome a concise and clearly expressed *outcome* to the discussions — perhaps a handout. In my own experience, the pooled outcome of plenaries can be pretty useless *as a product* — it is the process by which it is achieved that is valuable, though a handout can act as a useful *aide-mémoire* to this process.

A problem for the tutor is the temptation to respond authoritatively to student requests for direct guidance. 'How many hours should I put in each week?' can sometimes be answered from factual information from course descriptions, but the answer is probably not very helpful to the student. Asking back 'How do you decide when you have done enough?' might be more helpful. Being an 'expert' seems to be less helpful than being supportive and gently questioning.

Finally, about half of those who have adopted this approach make changes of their own. They alter aspects of the structure of the exer-

8

cises, provide their own materials, or design exercises on other topics using the same basic structure and principles. Once you have run a couple of exercises outlined in this book it will become easy to see how this can be done. As the approach takes a good deal of the pressure off the tutor it is relatively painless to try out new ideas. Chapter 3 is devoted to the design of exercises to meet your own particular needs.

CHAPTER 2

Six exercises to teach students to learn

This chapter contains instructions for six exercises, each designed to last one hour, laid out in a standard way in three parts. First there are some *Notes*. The Notes discuss the purpose and use of the exercise and raise some issues about the particular topic the exercise is concerned with. Second there are *Instructions*. The Instructions include the actual verbal instructions you would give to participants together with instructions about timing and the role you play in the exercise. The verbal instructions are not intended to be used verbatim, but merely to give a clear impression of the task you will be setting participants at each stage of the exercise. Finally there are *Materials*. These differ for different exercises and may consist of an example of the *outcome* of an exercise, a handout to be used *during* the exercise, or a stimulus of some sort (such as an actual student essay to be marked by participants) for the *start* of an exercise. Some of these Materials will not suit your needs and you will have to replace them with some of your own which fulfil the same function but are more suitable for your own particular context.

Each of the six exercises embodies an idea about using structured group exercises which can be used to meet other needs that you or your students may have. Chapter 3 discusses how you can use these ideas to design your own exercises.

Exercise One — How do we learn best?

Notes

This exercise is designed to act as an initial impetus to students thinking about their own learning. It seems to work well both as an introduction to the format of the group discussions and as an initial orientation to students to pay attention to, and value, their own experience of learning. It is an extremely reliable exercise and is usually very animated and involving. The reason for this seems to be that everyone has vivid experiences of learning, especially bad experiences of formal learning. These vivid experiences seem to be quite easy for people to draw on both to identify idiosyncratic characteristics of themselves as learners, and also to tentatively suggest general characteristics of 'good' learning. Even students who passively expect to be told how to learn can be surprised by how much they already know, from their own experience, about the conditions that foster 'good' learning and about what they can do to bring about those conditions.

If the substance of this session seems somewhat hazy and abstract then I suggest you read the Materials for this exercise. They consist of one student's input to the first two stages of this exercise and what he concluded from the exercise. I do not suggest that you use these Materials as a handout to your students at the start of the exercise unless you feel very unsure that they will be able to get going without some such model to prompt them. They are more to clarify the purpose of the exercise for you.

One possible outcome you may have to watch out for is participants who simply blame others for their bad experiences. Groups of teachers may tend to blame student laziness and stupidity and groups of students may tend to blame rotten teaching. If you can orient participants towards the role that they themselves play in learning situations this can help the exercise to be more constructive.

Instructions

*Working alone
(3 min.)*

'Think back to some past experience of learning — it could be at school, in sports, in a hobby, anything that was particularly awful — it may have been boring or humiliating, or you simply learnt nothing at all. Jot down a few notes on *why* it was so bad.'

11

(3 min.)	'Now do the same for a *good* learning experience — where you learnt a lot, were successful, enjoyed it and were interested. What was it that made learning so good? Jot down a few notes.'
Working in pairs (10 min.)	'Relate your experiences to each other, in pairs. Explain why your experiences were good or bad. What are the main *similarities* between what makes learning good or bad for you both? In what ways do you seem to thrive or suffer in different circumstances? Try and stick to basing your discussion in your own personal experiences rather than generalizing.'
Working in fours (24 min.)	'Form a group of four with another pair. From your pooled experiences of good and bad learning, can you see any themes arising? — things which for you tend to characterize good and bad learning in general. Each group of four elect a chairman who notes down what is said under two columns: "Things that lead to unsatisfactory learning" and "Things that tend to support and encourage very satisfactory learning". Note down as many things as you can under these headings.'
Working in plenary (20 min.)	'I'd like each group of four, in turn, to read out *one* item from its list. I'd like everyone else to ask that group to explain itself, to make the meaning of each item clear. Also, for each item, I'd like suggestions as to how that might affect the way you are learning here, in this institution, now.'

Continue until items or time are exhausted.

Materials

These are the experiences on which one student based his input to this exercise:

Thinking of a bad experience was easy. Even now, forty years after

12

I left school, I can remember my awful French classes. For every lesson we had to learn a list of vocabulary — just twelve or so words and what they were in English. I couldn't even remember half of them. I'd get two out of ten and have to call out my score so everyone would know. The teacher would be sarcastic: 'Two, eh Woodworth!' I could have died. I used to try and try, just staring at the words and saying them over and over, but nothing ever happened. I wasn't so bad at other subjects, just French.

-I suppose it was 'bad' because I didn't learn anything. Nothing. I don't remember more than a few words of French after *three years* of French classes twice a week. It was also horrible — I mean I dreaded classes and felt awful while I was trying to learn the words. It just seemed so hopeless and inevitable that I'd do badly.

Thinking of a good experience was much harder. I've always associated studying with having to do things I don't like, and doing badly. But there *are* things I've enjoyed finding out about, but I suppose I haven't thought of them as studying. A few years ago I got fed up with the 'holiday snaps' I used to take with my pocket camera and decided to get better at it. I didn't know how to choose a decent camera so I went to the library and took out a book on photography. It was a bit technical and off-putting and I told the librarian this and she looked up in a booklet and found an evening class on photography at the local school, and found me a *Which?* report on which camera to buy. The first evening at the class I felt a bit of a fraud with my shiny new camera. I thought all the others would be experienced and know about f-stops and film speeds and all those things, but it turned out that they were as naive as I was. Every week someone would bring in some photos they'd taken and we'd talk about what had gone wrong and the teacher, a young bloke, would make just a few gentle suggestions. He didn't overwhelm us with information. Just when we needed to know something, or someone wanted to try something new, like developing their own film, then he'd give us a bit of a talk. It was amazing because I can still explain all the processes involved in developing a film off the top of my head. No effort at all! I didn't miss a single evening class right through that awful winter.

This is what the student initially contributed to the discussion in *pairs*, in explaining *why* his experiences were good or bad:

Obviously I *wanted* to learn about photography, whereas I didn't have any choice about being at the French classes. And even though I did *try* to learn French vocabulary, it was only to pass the tests and avoid being shown up in front of my friends again. I didn't expect I'd ever *use* any of the French words. Now when I've been to France on holiday I feel I'd like to speak French just a little, but I've got a block about it. I couldn't bring myself to go to French evening classes.

I think some people aren't cut out to be linguists. I didn't seem to have any trouble remembering all the stuff about photography. I was more interested, and anyway I needed to know it if I was going to produce better photographs to take to the next class. The other thing was that at the photography class they were a really nice bunch of people. I didn't feel a fool asking them questions or admitting I didn't know something, though as I've already said, I was a bit apprehensive at first. When the year was over I went back to the library and that technical book made a lot more sense. I've read quite a lot since then and I've now got my own dark room at home.

Finally, this student's conclusions, after he had heard what others' experiences had been and how people were thinking about what these added up to, looked like this:

1. Simply trying to *memorize* stuff like French vocabulary can be a dull and fruitless task. Trying to understand something (like how to develop films) can be much easier and more enjoyable especially when you need to understand in order to be able to *do* something (like actually develop films). It can even make memory practically effortless.
2. Being *anxious* about learning (my two out of ten in class, and expecting others at the evening class to be experts) can really limit what you learn or even stop you starting.
3. Discussing what you learn (like with the photography class) seems to help. I think I get a lot from the social support.
4. Discovering things for myself and following up my own interests and being sort of actively involved in what I'm doing seems to make a lot of difference.
5. Learning what *you* want to learn is easier than learning what others want you to learn.

And there's loads of other things like it's easy to get overloaded with information (like my first encounter with the library book on photography) and starting *gently* can lead you to managing what you want in the end — like I managed to cope with the library book in the end.

Exercise Two — Organizing yourself

Notes

How organized students are is the one aspect of their studying that consistently correlates quite highly with examination results. Well organized students do better.

Some students, especially those straight from school or some other institution which limits personal responsibility, will have had very little experience of organizing themselves. For these students fairly simple and apparently obvious tips about planning and time management (like 'keep a list at hand of the tasks you've currently got to complete' and 'draw up a timetable of how you spend your week') may seem quite attractive and even be useful. For most people, however, ideas about how to be organized seem like lists of virtues. They all seem rather familiar, and thoroughly commendable but you also feel pretty sure that you personally will not ever become like that. How organized you are is a fairly fundamental part of who you are and how you are. Perhaps more than with any other aspect of learning, changing how organized (and by implication how hard working) you are involves feelings: threats and fears. Students can start to feel very incompetent and inadequate when confronted with just how marvellously organized and efficient it is possible to be. Students seldom discuss the topic. There is often even a social pressure to give an outward appearance of incompetence. In the subculture of Halls of Residence it seems quite common for students to have to pretend to have done no work, or to have no idea when an essay is due in, even if this is not the case.

For these reasons I tend to run exercises on being organized which start off with an attempt to get feelings about organization and diligence out in the open, and discussed, before possible practical solutions are suggested. One quick and effective way of getting at such feelings is to draw up a check list of statements you believe people would make about themselves, if only they had the courage. For example I once included the statement: 'I bet everyone here is cleverer than me' in a checklist handed out to the entire group of freshers at a university during their induction week. Overtly they were all looking cool, calm and collected. Every single student agreed with the statement.

The Materials for this exercise consist of a checklist of statements about being organized. The main benefits from this exercise seem to be concerned with making discussion of this topic legitimate; socially acceptable. It helps participants to recognize that their feelings and problems are not unique. The transition, towards the end of the exercise, towards discussing how participants cope with or avoid all these problems tends not to get very far. The notion that practical steps can be taken and that disorganization is not a wholly intractable problem, will come across. But little real progress is likely to be made about the details of practical steps and how to implement them. Further exercises, based around timetabling for example and backed up with contracts between students to try out particular ideas, are probably necessary for this. Chapter 3 discusses further how to back up exercises which, like this one, act as an initial stimulus to thinking, with more practical steps.

All the statements suggested with the Materials for this exercise are *negative* statements (e.g., 'I think that others do more than me'). This is because people seem to find it easier to say negative than positive things about themselves, and so it helps them to start identifying with statements and so thinking about themselves. However this can have, cumulatively, a rather negative and depressing effect. If you are worried about this happening then try including more positive statements such as: 'I get a real kick out of finishing things' and 'Deadlines give me a lot of energy to get down to things'.

As a final comment on this exercise, it is perhaps worth mentioning that its worst enemy is a character who attempts, with great enthusiasm, to persuade others that organization and planning are not a problem at all: 'Provided you do . . . (and here the character describes his or her own pet organizational technique) you'll be fine!' This is *not* useful to those students who *are* having trouble. If the character happens to be the teacher running the session this is disastrous. Those who manage to run their lives like the Swiss railway system seem to be in a particularly poor position to be empathetic and helpful to those of us for whom getting work done is a perpetual and irresolvable problem.

Instructions

Working alone
(5 min.)

'Read down this list of statements ticking those you feel apply to you. Alter statements so that they apply to you better. Note down any reservations or differences you have.'

'How many have ticked fewer than 5? Fewer than 10? Fewer than 15? 15–18?'

Working in pairs
(10 min.)

'Turn to your neighbour to form a pair and compare how you have responded. Have you responded the same for the same reasons? When you have responded differently, why is this?'

16

Working in fours *(30 min.)*	'Form a group of four with another pair. Briefly see where you agree and differ. Taking one statement at a time, ask yourselves: "Does this matter?" If you think it does, are there ways in which anyone in your group of four copes with or overcomes this particular problem? If particularly interesting or important ideas emerge, note down what they are for the plenary.'
Working in *plenary* *(15 min.)*	'I'd like each group of four in turn to take one of the statements you thought was particularly important and to tell the others what ideas emerged about it.'
	Continue until issues or time run out.

Materials

I don't think I work as hard as I could.
I couldn't tell you how many hours I put in last week.
I often seem to leave things like essays till the last minute.
I find it hard to get down to work.
I don't seem to be able to stick at a task (like reading through a chapter) for very long.
I think that others do more than me.
I don't find it easy to talk to others openly about how much work I'm doing.
I'm never quite sure what I've got to do next.
I sometimes take ages to 'get going'.
I'm not sure whether I'm doing enough or not.
I tend to flit from one task to another.
I seem to work better in some places than others.
I work rather irregularly, putting in lots of time one week and practically none the next.
I'm generally behind, sometimes several weeks behind schedule.
There is no way I could do all the work I'm expected to.
I'm not sure I always do the most important things first.
I'm not sure I'll be able to keep going right to the end of this course.
I don't have any sort of long-term plan for my work.

17

Exercise Three — Taking notes

Notes

This session uses the simple and useful device of asking students to undertake an actual learning task — in this case taking notes — and then just asking them to compare with other students how they did this. This enables differences between students to highlight the nature of the learning task — in this case some of the decisions about content and process which are involved in note taking and which might otherwise be taken for granted. Most inexperienced students, and even many experienced ones, are quite inarticulate about *why* they take notes in the way they do. The form of notes is often rooted more in habits taught at school than in any coherent rationale. Methods initially adopted to cope with copying information from the blackboard, which subsequently had to be rote-learned, are often carried over to other contexts where they are quite inappropriate.

Probably the most important thing to learn about taking notes is that it can serve a variety of functions in your learning. Different tasks make different demands, and different ends require different means. Let me illustrate what I mean by this.

First, specific tasks make different demands. Taking notes from a book makes different demands from taking notes from packaged learning materials (e.g., Open University Units) on the same topic. Books often require a good deal of structuring and summarizing in notes if their impart is to be encapsulated, whereas well-written packaged materials often do this structuring and summarizing for you, leaving note taking to perform other functions such as maintaining attention. Similarly, different lecturers make quite different demands on students. Some intend their lectures to be quite self-sufficient, and a student can get through the course without further reading provided *comprehensive* lecture notes are taken. Others intend their lectures to be no more than introductions to reading, and note taking may best perform the function of providing orienting instructions and precise referencing for this reading.

Second, different ends require different means. Students very often say that they take lecture notes in order to use them subsequently for revision or further work. But evidence suggests that students do not in fact look back at lecture notes as much as they would have you believe. One reason for this, I would suggest, is that their notes are not in a form which makes subsequent use very fruitful. The initial taking of the notes may have served the very useful function of maintaining attention for fifty minutes, but not met the end in mind. Also, students may say that they are taking lecture notes to help write an essay subsequently. But even a quick glance at their notes will show that there has been practically no consistent selection of information, let alone selection specifically for a known essay topic. If you want notes to help you achieve specific ends, then the notes have to be taken with those ends in mind. 'General purpose' notes may not help any *specific* ends to be met.

For these reasons it makes very little sense to talk about good and bad note taking *in general.* Understanding of the purpose of note taking can be most easily facilitated if the note taking is set in a real context with a clear learning task and a clear learning goal in mind. While it is possible to *simulate* particular tasks and goals it seems to be more effective to use 'real' contexts. For example, it is possible to give a mini-lecture from which you ask students to take notes — but half of them you ask to take notes for a subsequent multiple-choice question test on the factual content of the lecture, and half you ask to take notes for a subsequent group discussion of the issues raised by the lecture. Comparison of the sorts of notes the two sorts of tasks lead to could be used as the basis of an exercise. However, comparison of notes the students took from lectures on two different courses they are currently studying would be more likely to raise learning issues in a directly applicable and generalizable way. Once some basic distinctions about the purposes of notes have been made by your students you can go on and use these to examine note taking from different sources, in different contexts, and for different end results. But the nature of the distinctions may need to be rooted in your students' experience of their current learning rather than in artificial exercises if they are to be of use to them in understanding their current learning.

There are problems which may arise for this exercise which revolve around the degree of similarity or difference between students' notes. If your students have brought along with them notes from different lectures, different courses, or even different disciplines, there may be too many confusing variables to cope with. The demands of a civil engineering lecture may be so different from those of a philosophy lecture that in comparing their notes, students from these courses may merely decide that they have nothing in common and leave it at that. On the other hand, if students have all brought along notes from the very same lecture there may be too little variation to spark off controversy and thought about why the notes were taken in the way they were. This problem can be highlighted where lecturers have demanded that students note down whatever they write on the blackboard. Even at university this is depressingly common. This results in practically no variation in notes at all and your students are left wondering only if the lecturer's demand was sensible or not.

In either of these cases it may be helpful to have some specimen notes as a handout in order to highlight particular issues in note taking. The material for this exercise consists of sets of some social science notes. What the students who wrote them were trying to do, and what function such notes serve, either at the time they were taken or subsequently, can be left for discussion, or you can make your own tentative analysis as a model for how to go about thinking about note taking. A handout consisting of different notes taken from your students' own discipline, or even better from an actual learning task which all of them will have undertaken, would obviously work much better.

Ways of linking an exercise like this one into students' actual note taking behaviour are discussed in Chapter 3.

Finally, the task for pairs I have suggested here — of requiring each person to get to understand the other's notes sufficiently to be able to explain them to another pair when they combine into a four — is quite a useful one. It is particularly useful when you suspect students will take their own particular form of studying somewhat for granted and not really feel there is anything to be said about it. Another's lack of understanding and persistent questioning can get round this and draw out more than if the individuals were asked to explain their own notes.

Instructions

Working alone   This first stage involves students taking notes from some source — a lecture, book, film, tapeslide or audio cassette. This can simply involve the students' last lecture before coming to the exercise, a special note taking activity at the start of the exercise, or even, if this exercise is tacked on to the end of a normal lecture of your own, the students' notes from this lecture. The more recently the notes have been taken, the more vividly and completely will students be able to reconstruct how and why they were written.

Working in pairs   'In pairs, each of you in turn have a look at the
(10 min.)   other's notes and try to understand *why* they are written in the form they are. Which things

20

are included and which left out, and why? What will they be used for? Ask the other person whatever questions you need in order to understand their notes. Spend about five minutes on each set of notes. At the next stage you will be asked to explain and justify your *neighbour's* notes to another pair.'

Working in fours (20 min.)

'In fours, I'd like each of you in turn to try to explain your neighbour's notes to the other pair. Why are the other's notes different from your own? Do the others *use* their notes in the same way as you do? Find out! You are not allowed to describe your *own* notes unless your neighbour is unable to.'

Working in fours (15 min.)

'Still in fours, can you see from your four sets of notes what makes them either "good" and useful notes or "poor" and useless notes? Can you form a list of those characteristics you have identified which you think are useful and those you think you should avoid? Elect a chairman to write down these characteristics so you have a list ready to report at the plenary. You have about fifteen minutes.'

Working in plenary (15 min.)

'I'd like each group in turn to read out one item from its list. If what is read out is clear to the other groups and not contentious, then I'll write it up on the board under one of the two headings: "Good points about these notes" or "Bad points about these notes." If the points are unclear or contentious, I want others to clarify or object to them. I won't write anything up unless we can agree on it, and we are clear what it means.'

Continue until points are exhausted.

Materials

<u>Social Science</u>

<u>Lecture 3</u>   <u>17 Oct 1981</u>

Crime

1. <u>Quantity</u>

  1.1 Statistics

    1.1.1 Offences known to police

    1.1.2 Offences cleared up

    1.1.3 People found guilty

    1.1.4 Definitions vary

  1.2 Noticed

    1.2.1 Classification changes

    1.2.2 Police action varies

                — over time

                 — in diff. places

    1.2.3 Public attitudes change

  1.3 Crimes unrecorded

  1.4 Recorded as crime:

    1.4.1 Some more visible

    1.4.2 White collar crime

  1.5 Trends - based on statistics

2. <u>Causes</u>

  2.1 Definitions

    2.1.2 Laws define crime

Is crime getting worse?
(do I believe the Daily Express?)

Firstly, you can't really say crime is
getting worse 'cos can't tell how much crime
there _is_ :

   ⚹ official stats count odd things
      like who was found guilty,
      how many cases were 'cleared up' etc.
      but lots of crime is undetected,
      unsolved, unnoticed etc.

   ⚹ classifications differ — e.g.
      definitions of homosexuality &
      larceny. The police try less hard,
      the public care less.

WOT NO
CRIME?

   ⚹ lots of things don't count as crime — e.g.
      students smashing up their college isn't
      the same as Chelsea fans smashing shops
      & white collar crime is widespread but
      not detected (READ SUTHERLAND)

Secondly, even if you know how much crime,
you don't know _why_ :
      ⚹ what _is_ crime?

Exercise Four — Reading — using books

Notes

The sheer quantity of 'required' and 'recommended' and 'suggested' reading confronting most students must often seem to them rather overwhelming. In most courses it comfortably exceeds the quantity of new and unfamiliar material which one might reasonably expect them to be able to read thoroughly and assimilate. There is sometimes a realization of this difficulty by those recommending the reading when instructions take the form: 'You don't have to read all of this book, just have a look at it.' Unfortunately 'having a look at' a book is often something that inexperienced students do not have much familiarity with. It can come as a revelation that a book may contain only one or two central notions, and that most of the book consists of elaboration of, evidence for, and implications of, these notions. These basic notions might be contained within the blurb on the dust jacket, and it is often possible to get a fairly accurate idea of what a book is about in a few seconds. One of my students was so taken by the idea which arose in this exercise − that one can work through books usefully by reading only the first and last paragraphs of each chapter − that he promptly devoured five of his set books in one evening in this way!

This session is intended to explore the possibilities of using books in new ways.

Some students will be enormously resistant to the notion of not reading a whole book from cover to cover, *carefully*. They seem to feel that it does not do justice to the author or the ideas expressed if anything is missed out. They may even feel that it is not possible to understand the ideas properly unless the entire book is read. Even a demonstration of the effectiveness of very quickly skimming a book, and the recognition that others think it perfectly acceptable to use books in a cavalier manner, may not be enough to change such students' habits, so insecure do they feel if they miss anything out.

This exercise uses the device of getting students to do something which they might well *not* normally do. They might even baulk at doing it, believing it to be impossible. In everyday studying there is very little incentive and a good deal of risk involved in trying out a completely new way of going about a learning task. In exercises such as these it is relatively *safe*, and so it can be very rewarding − and even exciting − to students to be asked to do something completely new. In this case students are asked to extract the guts from a book first in two minutes, and subsequently in another ten minutes. The first notions you have of what a book is about make an enormous difference to how

24

you go about reading it, and what sense it makes to you. This exercise focuses on how these first notions are gained.

For Materials for this exercise I suggest you choose any reasonably structured book — a book which is recommended reading for a course your students are studying for example. It must be far too long to read in the time available but still have some reasonably coherent message which it is possible to extract. A book of readings, literature, or a scientific textbook would *not* be suitable.

However, I have offered some Material. This Material is not for the exercise for which I have given Instructions here, but for a similar one on reading short articles. It is easy to use much the same format for this as for the exercise I have described on using books. I would usually stop students unexpectedly after one or two minutes, after having initially told them they could have ten minutes, in order to identify their conventional way of starting to read, and to highlight the importance of the first impressions one gains for subsequent reading. The Material I have offered for this exercise is an article about exactly this reading issue, and would probably make interesting reading for you, even if you do not use it for your students.

Instructions

Choose as material any reasonably structured book — suggested further reading, for example, which is far too long to 'read' but has some reasonably coherent message (i.e., not a book of readings).

Working alone *(2 min.)*	'Imagine you are about to attend a tutorial on this book. You only have *two minutes* to check out what it is about before the tutorial starts. Off you go!'
(2 min.)	'OK, now write down what you think the book is about — as much as you have gathered in your two minutes. Don't "cheat" by looking back at the book.'
Working in pairs *(10 min.)*	'Compare what you have written down, and compare *how you found it*. Do you think you've got to the heart of it? Don't "cheat".'
(2 min.)	'I'm going to give you another *ten* minutes, now, to make what you can of this book, but

before you start, just suggest a few "plans of action" to each other. How are you going to tackle it?'

Working alone
(10 min.)

'OK, you are going to have to explain what you think the book is about to a *different* person after you've had ten minutes to work on it. Off you go.'

Working in pairs
(10 min.)

'Form pairs with someone different. Taking it in turns, one of you explain to the other what you now believe the book to be about. How did you gain that understanding? Do you both understand the same thing? Did you both look at the same parts of the book?'

Working in fours
(15 min.)

'Share your understanding of the book. What were the *best* ways (and the worst ways) of gaining that understanding? Did your initial one-minute scans affect the way you used the book? Elect a chairman who notes down good ideas about understanding the book quickly.'

Working in
plenary
(10 min.)

'Each group, in turn, explains one good way of getting to grips with the book in a short time. Did other groups use those methods?'

Continue till items are exhausted.

Materials

(for an exercise on the reading of short articles)

'Students' use and misuse of reading skills'
by William Perry*

Mr President, twenty years ago this Faculty undertook an experiment to see if some of its students could be taught to read better. Since the Faculty was then something of a pioneer in such an enterprise, it would seem appropriate that it should receive, after two decades, at least a report of progress — the more so because the work now concerns not the correction of disabilities of a few students but

*Perry, W. 'Students' use and misuse of reading skills', *Harvard Educational Review,* vol. 29, 1959. Copyright © 1959 by President and Fellows of Harvard College.

the direction of the abilities of a large proportion of the freshman class.

The students of this college are reputed to spend a good deal of time reading. In fact, a student sits with his books for nearly a thousand hours each year. The Faculty has a deep concern that these hours be fruitful. This concern is evident in the wording of assignments, in the layout of instruction in each course, and in the conversations of teachers with their students. It was this same concern that started the original experiment in reading improvement in 1938. The experiment began with a rather mechanical emphasis. It consisted of an instructor, whose main job was to run a projector for the first Harvard Reading Films, and some thirty student volunteers, hopefully the worst readers in the freshman class (and at that time there apparently were some freshmen who for Harvard's intents and purposes found it hard to read at all). The class met for about 18 to 20 sessions and engendered enough enthusiasm to become, like many an experiment, a kind of annual fixture, this one known as the Remedial Reading Course. Each year freshmen as they arrived in the fall would take a reading test and those who scored lowest would be informed of their plight and allowed to volunteer for the continued experiment.

When the Bureau of Study Counsel took over the actual instruction in this course in 1946, we met with thirty depressed-looking volunteers one evening in a basement class-room somewhere. Not knowing really what we were up against, we gave them still another reading test of a standard sort and discovered that every single one of them could score better on this test than 85% of the college freshmen in the country. We felt that to be useful to these people in their genuine dissatisfaction we were going to have to take a new look at the reading improvement game. We therefore abandoned the word 'Remedial' for the course and upgraded the material until it could jar the teeth of the average graduate student. Then we threw the doors open.

The amount of enthusiasm that exists in this community to read better − or if not better, then at least faster − is evidenced by the fact that we soon found ourselves with nearly 800 people enrolled in the course. When we examined the roll, we found that we had some 400 freshmen from Harvard and Radcliffe, 100 upperclassmen, 230 graduate students from the various schools, especially that of Business Administration and two professors − from the Law School.

Although the fees paid by these multitudes looked very attractive on the budget of a small office, we came to feel this was stretching our energies too far. We have subsequently cut the class in half and have been trying to make some sensible system of priorities whereby we might offer first chance on seats to roughly that third of the freshman class that might be most likely to benefit from this kind of instruction. In trying to find out who these people might be, we have turned up some observations about freshmen which may be of interest to the Faculty.

One wonders first of all why students who read, on tests, as well as these do, should want to attend a reading course at all, much less one that meets daily at 8 o'clock in the morning. Of course a number come in hope of magic — some machine they've heard of that will stretch their eyes until they can see a whole page at a glance. This is understandable. Freshmen are deprived rather abruptly of the luxury of thinking that reading is something they can finish, and are confronted instead with an infinite world of books in which they sense that they may forever feel behind, or even illiterate.

But year by year it has become more apparent that what the students lack is not mechanical skills but flexibility and purpose in the use of them — the capacity to adjust themselves to a variety of reading materials and purposes that exist on a college level.

What they seem to do with almost any kind of reading is to open the book and read from word to word, having in advance abandoned all responsibility in regard to the purpose of the reading to those who had made the assignment. They complain consequently of difficulty in concentrating and feel that they have 'read' whole assignments but are unable to remember anything in them. We have therefore shifted the emphasis of the reading course away from mechanics over to an effort to shake students loose from this conscientious but meaningless approach to their work. We have found that if they can be persuaded of their right to think, even though reading, they can then develop a broader and more flexible attack on the different forms of study and put their skills to meaningful use even on long assignments.

In offering freshmen priority on seats in the course, therefore, we have naturally wanted to know about their flexibility and their sense of purpose in reading. This is a hard thing to measure. To make some estimate of it we designed a new kind of reading test — as reading tests go it may really be rather peculiar — and presented it to the freshmen of Harvard and Radcliffe when they arrived this September. We suspected the students might learn more from it than we would, but this seemed a legitimate chance to take. I should like to describe this test and to tell you what the students did with it.

First of all, instead of the usual short passages which appear on reading tests, we presented students with thirty pages of detailed material — a complete chapter from a history book. We asked them to imagine they were enrolled in a course entitled The Growth of Western Institutions. We asked them to picture themselves sitting down of an evening to study one assignment in this course — this chapter entitled "The Development of the English State, 1066–1272'. They were to suppose that they had two hours ahead of them for this work, but that after all, they still had their French to do and some Chemistry to review before they went to bed. At the same time, they were to imagine that in this course an hour-examination would be given in about a week on which they would be asked to write a short essay and to 'identify' important details. We told them to go ahead about their reading in whatever way they thought best and to take notes if they wished. We told them this was a test of what they derived from the early stages of their study of regular assignments and that in about 20 minutes or so we would stop them and ask them questions appropriate to their particular method of work. We then turned them loose.

Twenty-two minutes later we stopped them and asked them what they had been doing. If they reported that they had been reading from the very beginning and going straight ahead into the chapter — whether rapidly the first reading, or carefully with a more rapid review in mind — we gave them regular multiple-choice questions on the chapter as far as they had gone in it. Up to this point the test was fairly standard, and we can report that the vast majority of the students, over ninety per cent of them in fact, reported that this was exactly what they had done. We can report that their rate of work in this particular approach was astonishing and their capacity to answer multiple-choice questions on detail was impressive. Some of them had read as many as twenty pages of very detailed material and were able to answer accurately every sensible question we could ask them about the detail.

The freshman class — as far as we could see — of both Harvard and Radcliffe, consisted of a most remarkable collection of readers — in the narrow sense of the term. The showing is most remarkable because, of course, these ninety per cent of the class were going at this chapter in the hardest way imaginable.

Let me explain what I mean. The chapter in question is an admirable piece of exposition, but like many admirable chapters it makes no initial statement of its aims, and it takes a little while to get going. And as a consequence, the reader who begins at the beginning with the Battle of Hastings and reads word by word is likely to find himself at page three hopelessly bogged down in the shires, the hundreds and the marches of Anglo-Saxon England. And after ten minutes or so, this was just where the students reported themselves to be. What we were interested to determine was how many students in the face of this burden of detail, the purpose of which was not clear, would have the moral courage — or should we call it the immoral courage — to pull themselves out and look at the ending of the chapter. Or even to survey the entire marginal gloss set out like sign posts page by page. The very ending has a bold flag out beside it which says — 'Recapitulation'. As a summary paragraph we doubt that we have ever seen a better one. From a half minute of study of this paragraph the whole development of the chapter becomes immediately clear to a reader and puts him in a strong position, not only to select among details as he reads them, but also to remember, for their meaningfulness, the details he would need to support an intelligent discourse.

Out of these 1500 of the finest freshmen readers in the country only 150 even made a claim to have taken a look ahead during twenty minutes of struggle with the chapter. And the vast majority of these seemed to have looked ahead only to determine how long the assignment was.

We asked anyone who could do so to write a short statement about what the chapter was all about. The number who were able to tell us in terms that had something to do with the growth of institutions, was just one in a hundred-fifteen.

As a demonstration of obedient purposelessness in the reading of 99% of freshmen we found this impressive. We had been looking for the one-third of the class most in need of our beneficent instruction and we had found just about everybody. We tried to find out if the students had behaved this way simply because it was a test — they reported no, that they always worked this way. When we pointed the ending out to them, some said, 'You mean you can sometimes tell what a chapter is about by looking at the end' and others said, 'O Lord, how many times have I been told!'.

Told or nor, after twelve years of reading homework assignments in school they had all settled into the habit of leaving the point of it all to someone else. We knew from our own efforts to teach independence of approach in reading that students find it hard to hear us even when the sheer bulk of college work could be handled in no other way. And we supposed that school-teachers had an even harder time of it. We were therefore prepared to find this widespread passivity of purpose; we wished to go beyond this and to identify those students whose misconceptions of reading involved something worse, a positive misconception of aim, a notion of the purpose of reading so at variance with the goals of Harvard that they might be especially slow at learning from their college experience. We had therefore added another turn to our test.

We asked students to imagine further that in their imaginary course an examination had been given on which an essay question had appeared. This question (which we hoped was a proper-type Harvard essay question) reads: 'From 1066—1272, the Norman and Angevin Kings laid the foundations of English self-government both by their strengths and by their weaknesses.' Discuss. (Twenty minutes). We then presented them with two answers, purporting to have been written by two students. The first of these was a chronological reiteration of the chapter by a student with an extraordinary memory for dates and kings and no concern for the question (or for any intellectual issue at all, for that matter). We calculated that no instructor with a shred of compassion in him could give this answer less than a C— even though it might deserve less. The second essay answer, shorter, and with hardly a date in it, addressed itself stringently to the issues posed by the question. We supposed this answer to be worth a B+, or perhaps an A— to a relieved instructor.

In validating the test, we had then begged the assistance of the chief section man in a real course, not wholly unlike this imaginary course of ours, and asked him to grade the essays. Of the first, he said that he really couldn't give the student a D because he had worked so hard; of the second we were pleased to hear him say that this was obviously an A student, even though all he was going to get on this essay was a B+.

To the freshmen, then, we presented on the test these two answers without reporting their value and asked them to state which of the essays was the better, which the worse, and to give their reasons. We are happy to say that on this they did quite well. Only two hundred students graded the better essay the worse, and only two hundred more gave the wrong reasons for the correct grading. This means that, on this particular measure, only a rough third of our freshmen showed themselves to be headed toward the wrong goals. Very possibly, were this same test to be given later in the year, the percentage would be much less. But we have experience to support that the tendency persists − often tragically.

These then were the students to whom we turned our attention. Until such students revise their sense of the purpose of reading, an increase in effort is likely to produce only worse results. Oddly, we have as yet found nothing else to distinguish them from other people. The number of them who come from public schools as against private schools is exactly the same as for the class as a whole, and they are by no means the least intelligent members of their class. We are eager to find if we can learn more about how they get their misconceptions. We hope that the Reading Course may help to turn some of them around. Perhaps the test itself helped; the section man who helped us with the test was quick to point out its instructional possibilities, and we gave the text and essays to the students to take with them, together with a page of comments. It was encouraging to have to thread one's way afterwards through knots of students working over their papers.

What might the faculty conclude from all this. As the faculty's agent in this area. I can report my own conclusions from this twenty-year experiment.

1. It appears that most students can learn to read better.
2. The instruction that assists them to do so does not center in the mechanics of reading. The mechanics of reading skill are inseparable at this level from the individual's purpose as he reads. If you train someone in mechanics alone, he drops right back into his old habits the minute he picks up an assigned text.
3. The possession of excellent reading skills as evidenced on conventional reading tests is no guarantee that a student knows how to read long assignments meaningfully. The fact that the Admissions Committee is providing students to higher and higher ability should not lull the Faculty into feeling that at last it does not have to teach students how to study. In fact the responsibility is

only the greater, for these students have the ability to muddle through assignments the wrong way and still get that wretched C−.

4. There can be no general rules for teaching the exercise of judgement in reading. Such judgement requires courage, and courage cannot be taught by rule, it can only be dared, or redirected, in ways appropriate to particular subjects and learning tasks. To be sure, the reading of conflicting authorities is a fertile ground for young courage, and an excellent exercise in reading skill. And a C− for the attainment of useless knowledge is perhaps less of a kindness in the long run than congratulations for effort and a clean E for expending it in the wrong game. However, the individual instructor in his own course remains the best judge of how to set up his assignments so that they demand a redirection of effort toward effort and away from ritual.

5. A short separate course of general instruction, like the Reading Class can be of some contributing value, if only because it offers a moment's freedom to experiment without the threat of failure. But its limits are very clear. In such a course we can only dramatize the issues, and this only in the area of very general expository reading. We can refer only briefly to science and must leave literature explicitly alone.

We feel, too, that only a narrow line of spirit divides such instruction from an invitation to mere gamesmanship. We sometimes worry, in teaching method without content, lest students gather that we recommend a glance at the ending of chapters and at nothing else. (We do dare students to suppose that even this is sometimes appropriate.)

I should like to be able to report, in conclusion, that when we do succeed in introducing students to the rigors of thoughtful reading they are invariably grateful. I must confess, a bit ruefully, that this is not always the case. I have here a description of this kind of instruction in a student's words. To assist us in developing the course we have occasionally given the students a questionnaire at the end, and this one of a year or so ago was a real up-to-date Social-Science-type, questionnaire: open ended at the beginning, pointed at the end, and all. It says here, 'What did you expect when you came to this course?' Big space. 'What do you think about it now?' Big space. On the other side a lot of specific questions. We did not ask students to sign their names, only to enter the scores they made at the beginning and end of the course.

This student's scores when he came to the course showed him to have derived only a D− kind of understanding from considerable study of the material. At the end he was obtaining a straight A understanding in one-third of the time. I remember settling back with this one in anticipation of those comments that a teacher so loves to hear − but not at all. He was furious. 'What did you expect when you came to this course?' 'I expected an organised effort to improve my reading.' 'What do you think about it now?' 'This has been the sloppiest and most disorganised course I have ever taken. Of course, I have made some progress, but this was due entirely to my own efforts . . .'

Exercise Five — Writing

Notes

In the original booklet on which this volume is based I devoted *four* exercises to different aspects of writing. It is when students are being *active* and *constructive* in their learning, and especially when they are writing, that their purposes and their conception of learning and of the whole intellectual enterprise they are involved in, become most apparent. Because of this it is through writing exercises that I find that I can have most impact in helping students to reconceptualize their learning and to reorient them towards new learning goals. The exercise I have chosen to give full Instructions and Materials for here is explicitly concerned with what writing is *for* and is called 'The writer's intention'. I have also included brief notes, but no Instructions or Materials, for three other exercises on writing which are concerned more with the mechanics of communication skills than with the purposes of studying.

A. The writer's intention

Students understand what essays are for in very different ways. They are trying to achieve very different sorts of things when they set out to write essays. They have different *intentions* when they write. This is a very hard notion to explain to students in the abstract, but very easy if concrete examples can be given to illustrate what sort of written outcomes result from different intentions. It is possible to carefully choose pairs of students' essays to illustrate the particular difference of intention you are most concerned with — or even to write your own.

The pair of short essays offered here as Material have been written in strikingly different ways. Although the students who wrote them both attempt to answer the same question their essays embody quite different notions of the nature of the task of essay writing. Two sorts of somewhat distinct factors may be involved in these different notions. First there may be differences in the conceptions of learning in general which underlie these students' intentions. I am referring here to the sorts of differences in conception discussed in Chapter 5. These sorts of differences would tend to lead to these students tackling all essays, whatever the context, in a similar way. Second there may be differences in the way these students understood the specific assessment requirements of the course they were studying. Wherever this pair of essays has been used with a group of academics it has led to disagreements amongst academics about which is best because they disagree about what assessment systems should be assessing. Both of these sorts of issues: about the goals of learning and about the criteria of assessment; are raised by this exercise. Because the variety of issues raised can be so broad it may be helpful, if the size of your student group permits it, to lead the pooling of points on the plenary into a general discussion of the purpose of essay writing. I tend to try to emphasize issues to do with students conceptions of the goals of learning, as the next exercise also raises issues about assessment.

Instructions

Working alone
(20 min.)

'Read through these two students' answers to this question. Which answer is best, and why? In what ways do they differ?'

Working in pairs
(10 min.)

'Compare your comments. Which answer is best, and why?'

Working in fours
(15 min.)

'Pool your conclusions. Were these students trying to do the same thing?
Describe what you think each was trying to do.'

Working in
plenary
(15 min.)

'I'd like each group in turn to make a comment about one of the answers, and about what the student was aiming to do.'

Lead into a general discussion.

Materials

Assess the noise pollution problems caused by Concorde around airports

---

Answer 1

The sound limit at Kennedy airport, New York, is 112 PNdB*, and at Heathrow, London, 110 PNdB. The manufacturers of Concorde (Sud-Aviation and the British Aircraft Corporation) have promised that Concorde will range between 104 and 108 PNdB, depending on its weight at take-off.

At the start of Concorde operations at Heathrow, 21 of the first 35 departures exceeded 110 PNdB, and in the first eight months of operations 72% of the 97 departures exceeded 110 PNdB. Overall in 1976 there were 109 infringements of Heathrow's limit by Concorde. These measurements of Concorde were about 7 PNdB lower than during its early endurance trials. At the same time there were 1,941 infringements by subsonic jets. Concorde rarely features in the list of the ten noisiest take-off's each month at Heathrow, and subsonic aircraft at Kennedy have been recorded at 121 PNdB — twice the limit.

At Dulles Airport, Washington, Concorde has averaged 119.9 PNdB at take-off and 117.8 PNdB on landing. This is 12–13 PNdB higher than the averages for subsonic aircraft. The noise levels have been going down, and with them, the number of complaints. In September 1976 the average level was 121.3 PNdB and there were 186 complaints (29 of these to one take-off). In October the average was 117.4 PNdB and there were 101 complaints. During this time polls of opinion concerning Concorde's trial period at Dulles showed an initial opposition of 36.9% drop to 26.2%. In New York, opposition to Concorde landing at Kennedy has dropped from 63% in January 1976 to 53% in April 1977.

While 500,000 people are affected by aircraft noise in Washington, 2,000,000 are affected at Kennedy. It has been estimated that 400000extra people will be affected by noise if 80 Concordes serve 12 US cities. This represents a 1% increase. Bumps in the runway at Kennedy force Concorde to take off closer to heavily populated areas, but due to advanced flight control characteristics Concorde can begin to bank at an altitude of 100 ft. compared with an average of 480 ft. for subsonic aircraft, and so can turn away from heavily populated areas sooner after take-off.

*PNdB means Perceived Noise Decibels — a logarithmic scale of noise

Answer 2

Opposition to Concorde based on arguments concerning noise pollution takes two main themes. The first is concerned with the 'sonic boom' — a phenomenon of supersonic flight *unique* to Concorde amongst commercial aircraft. The second is concerned with noise levels around airports caused during take-off and landing. This second theme is common to all aircraft, and the issue at stake is whether Concorde is significantly noisier than subsonic aircraft.

Comparisons with other aircraft are complicated by the changing nature of jet fleets. Early jet aircraft (eg. the DC8 and 707) used turbo-jet engines, and whilst these have been quietened, they are much noisier than second-generation fan-jet engined aircraft (eg. DC10 and jumbo 747). Eventually these older aircraft will be phased out, but at the moment Concorde is being compared with them.

There are also problems of measurement. Objective measures (meters giving a reading in decibels) cannot give any impression of 'shrillness' or subjectively experienced nuisance. An aircraft giving higher decibel readings may not be experienced as 'noisier' by someone hearing it take off. Subjective measures also involve problems, as 'noise' is such a multi-faceted phenomenon, and different people use different criteria in assessing it. There are dangers, also, in questionnaire surveys of reactions of people living around airports. Average ratings of 'nuisance' change over time without any changes in objectively measured decibel levels or frequency of aircraft movements and so other factors must be involved. These factors can be political. Boeing took care to subcontract for parts for its SST at factories surrounding Kennedy airport, so that votes concerning whether SST's should be allowed to use the airport would be influenced by residents concerns for their jobs! Workers at Filton and Toulouse would hardly try to ban Concorde landing near their homes, however noisy it is!

Finally, there is a variation in recorded noise levels dependent on the skill of the pilot, and load factors of the aircraft. Subsonic aircraft have been measured at twice the legal noise level, struggling to take off with heavy loads in adverse conditions. Concorde has been flying under-loaded, with skilled pilots, who have even been reported banking away from noise monitors.

Given this variety of problems, it would seem likely that Concorde causes even more noise pollution than data suggests, and that in comparison with subsonic jets will become comparatively worse as time goes on.

B. *What makes for a good read?*

One aspect of essay, report, and examination writing which distinguishes them from other forms of writing is that they are formally assessed. As a consequence it is common for students to leave *all* the evaluation up to the marker and to abandon all responsibility for its quality. It is very common for students not to read their work at all after it has been completed. They often do not realize that they have many perfectly valid criteria for judging their own (and their colleagues') writing. It is through developing these criteria and bringing them to bear on their own writing that they can alter and improve their own work.

This is not to say that all their criteria are appropriate. Students often imagine that it is the degree of sophistication of an essay — in terms of its liberal use of terminology, complex and tortuous phraseology and 'journalese' in general, copied factual information and so on — which determines the grade it will receive. In fact, of course, one's response when reading is heavily swayed by mere 'readability'. A clear simply expressed piece is generally better received than a piece whose structure is so complex the ideas cannot be recognized however good they may be. Students' misunderstanding of the nature and importance of originality in essays is another problem.

The purpose of this exercise is to draw out students' own criteria for judging writing by getting them to *mark* an essay and to write comments on it; students then compare their marks and comments and by discussion in groups try to arrive at some general criteria which they are jointly using to judge the essay. At the plenary these criteria are pooled and displayed on a board for discussion.

By and large the idiosyncratic and misconceived criteria drop out as students combine into larger groups and attempt to reach consensus, and the final pooled lists of criteria look *very* similar to those of academics marking the same essay. Usually students give an essay a *lower* mark than academics and are not so forgiving and able to recognize strengths. By this process students should gain some confidence that they do have valid criteria which they can then apply to their own writing.

There are also several subsidiary outcomes from such a group essay marking exercise, any one of which could be emphasized in instructions or the final plenary if it was felt to be particularly important.

First, students get a first-hand experience of what it is like for their teachers to mark essays. The tedium and annoyance that a blatantly cribbed hack piece of work in terrible handwriting can induce can readily be induced in students too!

Second, it can improve students' use of teachers' feedback. After they have attempted to make comments on the essay, you can ask them to imagine that the essay is in fact their *own* and that they have just got it back from their tutor. How do they feel about the comments? What are they going to *do* about them? Generally, of course, students are appalled at the comments they themselves have written and start to gain a better appreciation of the difficulties involved in giving useful feedback, and of some of the intentions behind comments. Students have sometimes said they will take much more notice of their tutor's comments after this exercise.

Third, students can be encouraged to take more responsibility in their own learning by this sort of evaluation exercise. It is one of Carl Rogers' (1969) fundamental principles of learning that independence is facilitated when self-evaluation is basic and evaluation by others is of secondary importance. The development of students' confidence in their own evaluative criteria engendered by this exercise can be followed up by requiring students to mark and comment on all their own written work *before* it is submitted for formal assessment.

The choice of Material for this exercise is crucial. Teachers have a tendency to choose superb essays as examples for exercises. Very often such essays can be so different from students' own moderate efforts, and seem so far beyond their ability, that little of value is learnt. Instead it seems to help to use an ordinary essay which is perhaps patchy in quality with both good and poor characteristics. Also if the handwriting and style of expression are *too* impenetrable and the ideas expressed *too* obscure, then too little will be available for comment and discussion. It may be worth showing an utterly cryptic essay as an example, but not as the material for a marking exercise. It is also important that the essay is written about subject matter which is familiar to the students and about which they care. An obvious source is one of the student's own recent essays, perhaps with the name, or even the handwriting, removed to maintain anonymity.

C. Explaining in writing: a sense of audience

Mere egocentricity is enough to make many people's explanations opaque. But, in addition, writing an essay on a subject about which your *only* reader knows a great deal more than you is a very odd task. Because students are aware of their tutor's mastery of the subject matter, it is quite common for them to assume that their reader has no needs at all — that, however they write, they will be understandable. This lack of recognition of tutors' needs as readers can lend to incomprehensibly written assignments in which assumptions the student has made about the reader's ability to understand statements and arguments are ill-founded.

The purpose of this session is to make some of these kinds of assumption explicit in a very simple task — that of giving written instructions. Suppose I were to ask a student to give me instructions how to reach the nearest bus stop from the room we were working in. His instructions might involve many assumptions about how well I knew the building I was in, and the surrounding streets — and even that I knew left from right! And because of the simple practical nature of the task, these assumptions would soon become apparent, especially if the student compared his instructions with those of other students, who would inevitably have made different assumptions. Other needs I might have in following these instructions may become clear too. If the logical steps in the instructions were too big, I might get lost. If they were too small I might get bored. I may want to check that, so far, I am still right. ('At this point you should be looking at the entrance'). It may be very useful to have an overall orienting instruction ('The bus stop is in the direction of the window') or some idea of the plan of the instructions so that I can use just those bits I need ('If you know how to get to the front entrance, skip to instruction No. 10'). It is relatively simple to then translate the lessons learnt into terms applicable to writing reports and explaining arguments in essays.

This exercise simply involves asking students working alone to write some instructions or directions, and then allowing them to compare and combine their instructions in pairs and then in fours, employing only the best devices at each stage. The plenary is used to identify the characteristics of these effective devices and to discuss their relevance to essay and report writing.

D. Writing — being flexible

There are many useful exercises which can be undertaken around the sheer mechanics of writing — the simple blocks which prevent us from writing more quickly, fluently and clearly. One such block is to do with our reluctance to abandon unpromising forms of explanation or description that we have adopted. If you observe someone writing it is likely that you will see their pen hovering hesitantly over the page for very much longer periods of time than you see it busily writing. One reason for this seems to be that we write ourselves into corners and then have a lot of trouble getting out of them. Many is the time I have written a paragraph, or even merely a first sentence, and it has led me into a cul-de-sac. I have struggled with difficult arguments or phrasings for ages in an attempt to get back into the line I had originally intended. All I in fact needed to do was abandon my sentence, or paragraph or unpromising approach and start again, but it terribly difficult to do that. It seems a waste of effort, or it never even occurs to me to start again. It is very easy for me to imagine the way I am tackling my writing is the *only* way. And it is perhaps even harder for an inexperienced writer facing a new task to see that there is more than one way of perceiving the subject let alone more than one way of writing about it.

This is an exercise in flexibility — approaching a piece of writing in a number of different ways in an attempt to break the rigidity and narrowness which can make writing so slow and painful. It simply involves asking students to write briefly about something with which they are familiar — an article they have all just read or a lecture they have just attended. You can ask them to write only the introductory paragraph which will contain a summary of how the whole piece will go. After ten minutes stop them and tell them to start again, taking a completely different approach. Students may well protest but reassure them this is possible! Then allow students to compare their writing with each other so that they can see the enormous variety of approaches that could have been taken. Finally ask students to write one more paragraph, using some of the ideas which they have seen but which is different from the first two they wrote. This is doing little more than giving them practice at being flexible, but the experience of being *able* to take different approaches can really help to loosen up students' writing habits.

Exercise Six — Taking examinations

Notes

Examinations are such an emotionally-charged subject for most students that almost any opportunity to discuss them can lead to a great reduction in anxiety. A structured discussion in which students simply share the revision techniques they have found most useful in the past can work well, especially if the most promising techniques can be explored more fully at the end of the discussion. This might involve: students noting down their own favourite techniques for five minutes; sharing these in pairs for fifteen minutes; pooling the best in fours for twenty minutes; and then having twenty minutes to explore the implications of one or two of these techniques.

The exercise offered here is aimed at what is involved in actually sitting the examination itself. It gives students the chance to think about how to plan their time and tackle the examination paper sensibly while not under stress or time pressure. As *material* you will need a past examination paper, complete with any examination instructions, for a course your students are studying. If you have students from different courses, make sure that each group of *four* at the least, is working from the same examination paper.

The timings for this exercise are very tight. It would benefit from considerably longer, especially as exercises on examinations seem to have a cathartic effect and raise all sorts of powerful issues for students other than those strictly connected with taking examinations. It may take some guidance from you at the plenary, or even an additional exercise, to make the link between examination tactics and revision tactics.

Such a large part of examination performance is nothing to do with what students understand about subject matter that it is possible to run an exercise solely around these extraneous factors. If you have examiners' reports which identify what went wrong last year you can ask students to guess what the report commented on — what students do wrong that results in poor marks. Once their guesses have been pooled at a plenary you can hand out the examiner's report or a list of your own. My own 'general-purpose' list is included here as Materials. The important point about this list is that it is so obvious and apparently trivial that simply given as advice as what not to do it is likely to be ignored.

Instructions

Working alone *(5 min.)*	'Imagine you are in the examination room, and you are given this exam paper and told to begin. Go ahead, for ten minutes, exactly as if you were really doing the exam.'
Working in pairs *(5 min.)*	'Compare what you did with your ten minutes — was it different? Why?'
Working in fours *(10 min.)*	'Pool the tactics you adopted. What are the most useful things to do in the first ten minutes? What things are best avoided?'
Working alone *(10 min.)*	'Now go back and start tackling a question which *isn't* your best question (choose your 2nd or 3rd best) and start working on it. You have ten minutes to work on it. Don't try and finish your answer in ten minutes, just use it as the *first* ten minutes you'd spend on this answer.'
Working in pairs *(5 min.)*	'Compare how you went about starting to answer your chosen question.'
Working in fours *(15 min.)*	'Pool your tactics. What methods of revision would be best suited to the tactics you would choose to adopt?'
Working in *plenary* *(10 min.)*	'I'd like each group in turn to describe a promising way of tackling the paper, and going about answering a question; and to suggest what form of revision would be the best sort of preparation for that way.'

Materials

(These materials are *not* for the exercise for which there are instructions, but for an additional exercise discussed in the Notes.)

Things which students do which result in them doing badly in examinations:

- Turning up late and flustered — and so losing time.

- Not following the examination paper instructions about which and how many questions to answer and so answering questions which do not count and missing out questions which do count.

- Budgeting time between questions so badly that not enough questions are answered (e.g., three instead of four, throwing away twenty-five per cent).

- Misreading or misunderstanding questions through spending too little time deciding what is being asked for — and so answering a question which has not been asked.

- Reading whatever the question (whether 'Discuss . . .' 'Compare and contrast . . .' 'Evaluate . . .' or whatever) as: '*List* whatever you can think of about this topic in whichever order you can think of it. Make no attempt to organize your answer. Include only unconnected facts.

- Writing illegibly. This is *very* common. The more slowly an examiner is forced to read, by poor handwriting, the less chance there is that he or she can work out what an answer is saying.

- Using opinions and personal experience as a substitute for well-supported arguments. Abandoning all logic and intellectual rigour.

- Believing that sheer quantity will gain marks. In fact, the reverse can be the case — good points and arguments being lost in a welter of irrelevant detail.

- Forgetting that the first 50% of marks for an answer are relatively easy to obtain, the next 25% extremely difficult and the last 25% quite impossible — and so wasting time elaborating on already good or adequate answers instead of improving poor and inadequate answers.

- Trying to remember what they know about a topic, select what is relevant to a question, organize it into an answer and formulate sentences to express that answer *all at the same time* instead of in separate stages — and so producing partly irrelevant, disorganized, incomplete and incoherent answers.

- Failing to read through finished answers for grossly incoherent and incorrect passages.

- Panicking.

This is, of course, a partial list and you may wish to delete and add items to suit your own subject discipline and experience.

CHAPTER 3

Going beyond the exercises

This chapter is concerned with practical issues involved in going beyond the six exercises in Chapter 2. It contains three sections: 'Designing your own exercises'; 'Putting your own course together' and 'Limits to the approach'.

Designing your own exercises

People find it relatively easy to modify the exercises in Chapter 2, or to design their own, to meet their own particular needs. They all use the simple device of Andrew Northedge's structured discussion technique (1975, see also Chapter 7) to examine aspects of students' approaches to learning, and it requires no special expertise to employ this device in new ways. However, the six exercises in Chapter 2 were carefully chosen to illustrate different ways of using this discussion device and it may be useful here if I briefly identify and discuss these different ways.

Generating content

The most important variation is in the way the content of the structured discussion is generated. If you simply ask students to discuss how they go about their studying, they rarely have much to say. You need to use various devices to help them gain access to the processes, decisions, purposes and so on that make up studying. One of the best ways of doing this is to provide an immediate experience of studying and then to ask very specific questions about this experience. The exercise: 'Taking notes' does this, and it is a simple and reliable device which requires little of you, the teacher, to employ.

Variations on this device can be used to highlight particular aspects of the learning task. The exercise: 'Reading — using books' involves students undertaking a learning task they might not have undertaken before, let alone examined in detail, and so provides a novel experience. The other reading exercise suggested involves *interrupting* a learning task unexpectedly at a particular point — in this case very early on — in order to examine the importance of the first steps that are taken as a part of the task. The writing exercise 'Being flexible' gives students practice at going about a novel task *repeatedly* as a basis for discussion. The exercise described on tackling examinations *simulates* the learning activity — students are not asked to sit a real examination. But all these are simply variations on providing immediate experience as a basis for discussion.

A good reason for basing discussion in immediate experience is that if you ask students to discuss some aspect of their learning — their note taking, for example — *in general*, then the outcome tends to be somewhat vacuous generalities. If students' *past* experience is to be used as the content of the structured discussion, then it helps to limit the degree of generality by asking about very specific experiences. For example, the first exercise: 'How do we learn best?' does not ask students to generalize about how they think they learn best, but asks them to first recall and describe two specific experiences (one good, one bad), asks questions about these specific experiences, and attempts to base all discussion on these specific experiences.

Unless learning activities undertaken more than twenty-four hours before involved particularly powerful emotional experiences, it can sometimes be quite difficult to gain accurate and detailed access to the *process* of that learning activity without using various *recall* devices — ways of helping students to remember more. Video or audio recordings of tutorials, and even of lectures, can provide a very powerful and effective recall cue. When accompanied by non-directive questioning, as with the 'enquirer role' of Kagan's interpersonal process recall method (Kagan, 1975) it is possible to gain access to feelings and insights not otherwise available for analysis. However, sophisticated recall devices are not necessary for most purposes, and something as simple as a student's own set of lecture notes can be used to 're-create' the lecture.

Gaining access to students *feelings* about their studying can be quite difficult. The device used in the exercise: 'Organising yourself' of providing a checklist of feelings and personal statements can be effective in cueing students' own feelings and making expression of them easier. Questionnaires, checklists of statements, and even vignettes of carica-tured students can all work well to help students to articulate otherwise inarticulate and incoherent thoughts and feelings about their studying. Even study habits inventories designed to help teachers to diagnose students' study weaknesses (an activity criticized in Chapter 4) can be useful as tools of *self*-diagnosis, and to help students to conceptualize their own study methods.

For two of the exercises on writing ('The writer's intention' and 'What makes for a good read?') the content of students' discussion is not their own studying but their criteria for evaluating learning out-comes. The initial tasks require students to judge the quality of essays written by *others*. Using the outcomes of study activities produced by a third party can help to limit the inevitable *post hoc* rationalization of habitual and thoughtless forms of studying into which students can relapse when trying to analyse their *own* outcomes. It is possible to use a third party's essays, notes, laboratory reports, examination answers, and even personal accounts of tutorials or other learning activities, and ask students to evaluate them, in order to provide an input to a struc-tured discussion. It is possible to focus such evaluation by providing some contextual information. For example: 'This student has described a tutorial she attended and the role she played in it. She said that the reason she turned up to tutorials was to "make more sense of what the lectures were about". Given that this was her aim, do you think the things she did during the tutorial were the most appropriate or effective things she could have done?' – and to hand out a description written by yourself to highlight certain sorts of characteristic and unproductive tutorial behaviour.

Manipulating the structure

The basic structure of the exercises in Chapter 2 involves students working alone for a short time, working in pairs for a bit longer, work-ing in fours for the longest period of time, and then pooling some con-clusions and gaining an overview in a relatively short plenary. The rationale for this structure is discussed in Chapter 7. While there are some good reasons for keeping to this basic structure, there is plenty of scope for varying it to suit your needs.

The simplest form of variation is in the amount of time allocated to the different stages. Reacting to a checklist or a set of notes with which a student is already familiar may take only a couple of minutes, whereas marking an essay may take twenty. It is important not to rush

47

the first stage as the quality of subsequent discussion depends heavily on how deeply students get involved in the initial task. The time needed for discussion in pairs and fours may depend more on how well discussion is going than on the nature of the question or task that has been set.

No time has been set aside in the exercises in Chapter 2 for the discussion and formulation of practical steps which can be taken on the basis of what has been learnt in the exercises.

A second variation in structure concerns how *tasks* are structured within each stage. For example, in the exercise 'Taking notes' I have suggested dividing up the time spent in fours into two periods during which different questions are to be addressed. When it is felt that students may have difficulty drawing out principles or generalizations from specific experiences it can help to deliberately carve up the task to separate becoming familiar with the nature of the experience from drawing conclusions from it. Sometimes one task is too big to handle and it can help to divide it up, and to divide the time allocation up in order to emphasize the division of task.

A final variation, and one which many people adopt, is to go through the cycle — of working alone, in pairs, in fours and as a whole group — more than once. Some activities produce useful insights very quickly which can be put to good use almost immediately, and it can be ponderous and inefficient to spend a whole hour extracting these insights. In the exercise 'Using books' for example, even a very brief experience of trying to find out what a book is about in a very short time can lead to many good ideas and insights emerging which students are keen to employ straight away. This exercise uses pairs to raise some of these initial ideas and then puts students back to work on their own. The exercise 'Writing — being flexible' puts students through the cycle more than once as they get practice at undertaking a task and then ideas from comparing their experience with others before going on to get more practice.

The possibility of repeatedly putting students through the cycle seems an attractive one and appears to offer the opportunity of achieving more in a given time. However, it is very easy to go too far and make each stage so short that only superficial analysis takes place and only trivial outcomes emerge. Students who are used to spending an hour *just* listening, an hour *just* discussing, or an hour *just* working alone, can have difficulty enough adjusting to changing their role during one-cycle structured discussions without having to adjust repeatedly and perhaps before they have even settled into the role the last stage demanded. Teachers adopting structured discussions as a teaching method seem to try and pack in as much as possible to begin with before settling down to a less complex and frenetic structure.

48

Back-up materials

Sometimes the best-prepared exercises do not work all that well. This can be because students were not sufficiently engaged by the initial task to have worthwhile material to take to subsequent discussion. Students who are not used to questioning themselves about the way they study may find even very clear instructions difficult to understand and follow. They do not have a clear enough idea of what sort of things can be said about a set of notes, or a past learning experience, to get involved in thinking about it. On these occasions it can help to have some additional materials at hand to help students to conceptualize the task facing them in analysing their own studying. In the exercise 'How do we learn best?' I have offered an example both of what a student might use as *input* to the exercise, and what the student's personal outcome from the exercise might look like. I think examples like this can be enormously useful in helping students to recognize that a lot of analysis and progress can be made without any sophisticated language or specialist knowledge about learning.

An alternative way of providing such a model for the task you are giving students is to undertake a 'live' analysis yourself of, for example, the notes offered with the exercise 'Taking notes'. You could simply give a few off-the-cuff comments about what you see the function of such notes as being and highlight any strengths or weaknesses you may see. This would not be in order to identify the correct and incorrect way of writing notes, but to offer a model of how to approach thinking about note taking.

Sometimes what students bring to an exercise may not allow much scope for discussion. For example, they may all have written a very standard laboratory report to a very strict pattern, and brought this as a basis for discussion of writing reports. The lack of variation would limit the range of issues raised. It can be useful in these circumstances to produce your own laboratory report, written in a contrasting way, as a handout to introduce more variety, or, as with the exercise 'The writer's intention' a pair of selected reports which, by their contrast, raise the specific issues you wish to raise.

Putting your own course together

It seems that few people use just one of these exercises in isolation with their students. Most put several together into a longer 'workshop', or into a short course on a once-a-week basis. There are some very good reasons for doing this. Students' study habits are often very deep rooted and inflexible, and their conceptions of learning rigid and unquestioned. A one-hour exercise, however brilliantly conceived and executed, is unlikely to bring about immediate and radical changes by itself. The cumulative force of several exercises can, by repeatedly questioning the purpose and process of students' learning, make change much more likely. Students can come to see that it is not just their note taking technique which embodies particular purposes, but that a recognizable approach to learning runs throughout their reading and essay writing as well. Each exercise builds on students' overall awareness of their studying and reinforces new and difficult-to-grasp ideas. A regular period of time put aside to examine studying can help self-reflectiveness and self-evaluation become a habit. Students can become self-improving.

Interspersing these exercises with periods of normal everyday study, by running them once a week during term time, for example, brings with it extra advantages. A danger with intensive study methods courses, especially those run out of term-time, is that the lessons learnt are not so easily transferable to everyday studying. It can help this transfer enormously if students do some everyday studying between individual exercises. This helps in two ways. First it can provide a more immediate and realistic basis for students' discussion of learning experiences during the exercises. For example, if you have planned to run an exercise on learning from discussion next week, then you can ask your students to stop immediately after any tutorial, seminar or formal discussion group over the next week, and jot down some notes about what was good and bad about it, what role they personally played in its success and failure, and so on. Students then turn up to next week's exercise with a more comprehensive basis for discussion than had the exercise occurred in the middle of a day devoted exclusively to these exercises.

Second, and more importantly, it can provide an immediate opportunity to try out some of the ideas that have emerged in an exercise in order to see what the consequences are for learning. For example, supposing that a student were to discover, in an exercise on note taking, that several colleagues took few or no notes from a particular lecturer while he himself took copious notes. At the same time the colleagues said they were trying to 'get a feel for the ideas' while he himself was trying to 'get down as much as possible'. An obvious activity for this student to try would be to listen to this particular lecturer *without taking notes* in order to see if he got something different out of it from when conscientiously scribbling. However, even though the idea to undertake this activity might have come from the student himself and even though it would have considerable face validity because colleagues already did it, it is still not all that likely that the student would try it out and risk missing an entire set of lecture notes. What is required is some extra impetus, some extra practical arrangement, which will make such risk-taking experimental activity safe enough and worthwhile enough to undertake.

One way study counsellors have gone about tackling this problem is to arrange 'contracts' with students. This involves the student coming to an agreement with the counsellor about some practical change the student promises to bring about, or new activity the student promises to try out, before meeting the counsellor again to report back on how things turned out. The most articulate proponent of this way of actually getting students to change their study habits, rather than to be simply aware that alternatives exist, is Goldman, of the University of Reading (cf Goldman 1979).

However this sort of contract seems somewhat one-sided. The *counsellor* is not promising to do anything difficult, and it is largely only the student's dependence on and submission to the counsellor's authority that makes this sort of contract stick at all. Only a relatively insecure student lacking in self-confidence and self-direction is likely to undertake many such one-sided contracts. It is also a very time-consuming business, requiring the counsellor to formulate contracts on a one-to-one basis and to check on the fulfilment of these contracts on a one-to-one basis as well.

Less one sided, more economical of teachers' time, and more in keeping with the student-centred approach taken here, stressing students' independence and personal responsibility, is to encourage students to make contracts with each other, the outcome of which will be used as the basis of the next exercise, the following week. What the nature of the contract is, whether the students fulfil this, and so whether students bring anything with them to the next exercise is known only to the students themselves, their contractual partners, and the sub-group of four they work with the following week. The pressure not to let your pair group and colleagues down after having made an arrangement with them, is usually sufficient to encourage quite bold experimentation.

Let me illustrate how this might work with the student I hypothesized earlier who took comprehensive notes from a particular lecturer while his colleagues did not. Possibly after various suggestions, this student could form a contract with another to reverse roles for the next lecture in this series. The 'listener' would take comprehensive notes − to see what it was like to do so, and to make sure a set of notes was available if needed − and the compulsive note taker would listen, to see what it was like. They would have contracted to discuss the experience after the lecture and to see what they thought of the notes the 'listener' took. Their conclusions they would bring with them to the next exercise as their contribution to the initial discussion. At this exercise the first five or ten minutes would be devoted to exchanging experiences concerning the 'experiments' tried out as a consequence of the contracts made at the previous exercise. Students who did not fulfil their contracts would have nothing to contribute. There can be considerable social pressure not to do this without any intervention by the teacher whatsoever. It is not necessary for the teacher to know even whether contracts have been made or fulfilled, let alone what the contracts and their outcomes consisted of. In fact it seems to encourage students to take responsibility for this sort of personal growth if the teacher's authority is not involved in any way.

Sometimes such contracts are quite difficult to formulate in an acceptable way. Students are unlikely to have any experience of doing so, and it can be quite a worrying prospect. Teachers can be helpful here by making suggestions. For example our compulsive note taker might find the prospect of making a contract with a confident listener too challenging, and might not, in any case, trust the 'listener' to take an adequate set of notes from the lecture. Less confident students tend to stick together and make contracts with each other. One way to cope with this might be to suggest that one of a pair of compulsive note takers should listen for the first half of the lecture while the other should listen for the second half. Their notes would be combined to form a full set, and both would get the experience of just listening. This sort of perfectly reciprocal contract seems to work best where students are anxious and not too trusting. The teacher may need to be inventive and sensitive if contracts are to be made and fulfilled.

Such contracts can therefore be used to help make the transfer, of ideas and reconceptualizations which take place during exercises, to everyday studying. They can help the exercises to be based in realistic learning experiences instead of somewhat unrealistic games and simulations of learning experience. They encourage students to use each other as sources of ideas and feedback concerning different ways of learning, and help make concern for studying a legitimate social activity instead of a private worry,

Ideally, the more closely such a course of regular weekly exercises is built into the routine of studying the better. Very often timetabling and the availability of rooms make times like Thursday lunchtime or even the Wednesday afternoon sports time the only slots available for such exercises. They can then easily be seen as having low priority in the eyes of teachers, obviously outside the normal curriculum and patently not necessary. The allocation of a conventional timetabled slot and conventional teaching room helps legitimize and prioritize study

52

courses, as does their being 'advertised' as if they were a normal teaching and learning activity instead of something specially laid on by the medical service for struggling students. Being run by students' own teachers rather than counsellors or librarians obviously helps their legitimacy, too.

I have been told of courses which have been so integrated into conventional teaching that they are not perceived by students to be courses at all. Conventional lectures, tutorials and essay-writing tasks can all be modified and have built into them devices which encourage students to be reflective about the purpose and process of their study methods. The sort of intellectual development described by Perry (1970) which I discuss in Chapter 5 must be the goal of students' entire education, and it is absurd to relegate all students' development as learners to a course separate from their mainstream education.

Limits of the approach

The approach propounded in this book assumes that developments in students' study techniques take place in a useful and purposeful way when rooted firmly in developments in students' understanding of the nature of the learning tasks with which they are confronted. It is this development in students' understanding, and the reflectiveness, awareness and autonomy that it embodies to which this book is primarily addressed. However, several of the exercises in Chapter 2 are concerned more with technique than with understanding, even though they use a student-centred rather than a didactic approach to explore technique. Some areas of studying are so bound up with technique and simply knowing things, that a wholly student-centred approach makes less sense. A good example of this is the use of libraries. A good deal of what you need to use a library appropriately is concerned simply with information about the organization and layout of the particular library you use. There is still plenty of scope for the use of student-centred exercises to help cope with students' anxieties about using libraries, to help express a student's rather than a librarian's view of library use, and to link library knowledge with actual practice. However, it can be very difficult to design an exercise on library use without understanding how the library actually works, and also, without understanding the way libraries structure knowledge in the particular discipline in which students are studying. Simply telling students how libraries work and how the journal and abstract system is structured in your own subject will not help them much more than telling them how to take notes will help them with note taking. But running a totally non-directive exercise on library use will not get students very far very quickly either. There is simply too much specialist knowledge involved which, if it is not known or is ignored, will cause great difficulties. Library use is an area where, unlike most other aspects of studying, there are right and wrong ways of doing things which will either find you what you want or fail to find it for you.

Being able to use your library effectively is clearly to do with learning, but there are other aspects of studying which are similarly dependent on knowledge rather than underlying conceptions of purpose, but which are not to do with learning at all. I am referring here to the great wealth of academic conventions within which most higher education is framed. The acceptable and unacceptable turns of phrase in essays, the appropriate conventions of referencing, the structure of laboratory reports, and even the less tangible conventions concerning the expression of personal opinions and the position of originality, all make up a body of knowledge about studying which is vital to students' performance, but largely irrelevant to learning. If students do not become familiar with this knowledge, or ignore it, they will suffer in terms of their grades, though it is unlikely to affect what they learn in any important way.

Such academic conventions make up part of what has become termed the 'hidden curriculum' (after Snyder, 1971) — that is the curriculum which, while not the official curriculum, is the one to which attention must be paid if one is to succeed. For example, most students are heavily overloaded and it is quite impossible to do everything required. Learning what can be safely left out is learning about the hidden curriculum. Paying attention to some aspects of the hidden curriculum may mean little more than being aware, or being 'cue-conscious' (Miller and Parlett, 1974). But equally students can go far beyond this. Making a good impression on the teacher, recognizing the teacher's particular personal theoretical biases and preferences, learning to answer multiple-choice questions when the answer is not known, deliberately playing on quirks of the assessment system, and carefully spotting examination questions and ignoring all other subject matter; all these may have more effect on grades than the efficiency of study techniques and yet all have nothing whatsoever to do with learning. The extent to which students will be aware of the hidden curriculum and be able to distinguish between different demands made on them will depend on their overall sophistication as learners. Indeed the ability to make such distinctions is used as an indicator of students' development by Säljö (1976b — see Chapter 5). However, whether a course should set out to encourage students' attention to the hidden curriculum is a difficult ethical issue.

My own position is that students should be free to choose how to go about their studying. If a student is not aware of 'what counts' in his institution, then he is not free. How he chooses will depend on his overall orientation, and I have an obligation to help him explore the way his approach to studying will help him achieve his goals. To ignore the hidden curriculum and to pretend that only diligence and efficiency bring rewards is to lose credibility as a realistic source of help. But there can be a narrow divide between teaching students to learn and teaching students to play the game successfully.

The rationale for the approach

I have written the rationale, for the student-centred approach outlined in Part 1, in four stages corresponding to the four chapters in Part 2. The first stage involves examining the conventional approach taken to teaching students to learn, that is, *telling* students how to learn, for its validity and effectiveness. What is wrong with it helps point towards an alternative approach. But this book's alternative has been directed by two other influences: contemporary research into student learning, outlined in Chapter 5; and my personal beliefs about how people learn and change in general, stated in Chapter 6. A particular method of running tutorial groups was available as a form in which to realize this alternative, and this method is introduced and its own rationale explained, in Chapter 7. Together, these four chapters are intended to provide a conceptual framework which can be used to build on and go beyond the approach outlined in Part 1 and to use it in a creative way. Student-centredness is not simply a technique, it embodies assumptions and beliefs about how people learn. If it is to be used in more than a rigid, routine and desultory way, then these assumptions and beliefs need to be made explicit and form the guiding principles of its use.

CHAPTER 4

Why not just tell students how to learn?

By far the most common way of attempting to improve the way students learn is to give them advice. As Alex Main (1980) has pointed out, there are now over one hundred *How to Study* manuals in print in the English language. Every university bookshop stocks several of the more popular of these. So the obvious step to take, and the one most often taken, is simply to give some of this readily available advice to students. Unfortunately this is not always a very useful thing to do, and this section will attempt to explain why this is so. There are a number of assumptions which underlie study skills advice which this chapter will question in some detail. The first of these assumptions is that it is well known what study skills consist of.

Do we know what the necessary study skills consist of?

This would at first seem to be an unnecessary question. We all know that students need to be able to read effectively, take useful notes, write good essays, solve problems and so on. Unfortunately such an analysis does not take us very far. What, for example, does effective note taking actually consist of? Again, we might think the answer obvious. Not so. If we were to ask a room-full of successful academics to take notes from a lecture and then examine what they had done, we would find that they had all done something rather different, and that some people would have taken no notes at all. This is not merely a conjecture, I have used this as a demonstration on several occasions. The same is true of practically any aspect of study activity. Successful learners do different things and different techniques suit different people. More-over, even if we were to find one form of notes cropping up frequently, this would be an insufficient basis for advising our students to take notes in this way. While it is possible to observe what a note taker is writing down — the layout, use of abbreviations and so on — it is extremely difficult to reveal the processes of selection of subject matter, its transformation and organization, which determine *why* particular items are written down. Two sets of notes of outwardly similar form can have been produced by entirely different processes, for entirely different reasons, and with completely different learning outcomes. Recommending only the outward form notes should take is utterly unhelpful to students.

It is not even the case that note taking in general has been shown to benefit learning. Numerous studies have shown note taking to be associated with no better learning outcome than *not* taking notes (e.g., McClendon, 1958, Eisner and Rohde, 1959, MacManaway, 1968) or even for note taking to produce *poorer* learning outcomes (e.g., Peters, 1972, Crawford, 1925). Hartley and Trueman (1978) have even reported a negative correlation between amount of note taking and degree classification — the more notes were taken, the poorer the learning outcome. Negative, or no-difference, findings are however not the only findings on the benefits of note taking, and there is no clear indication whether note taking *in general* is useful. Howe (1977) has argued that those studies which *have* shown beneficial effects of note taking have done so following prolonged lectures where note taking has performed the function of maintaining attention.

It might be, we could argue, that the real benefit of notes is at the time of revision. Again, evidence would not support us. My own experience, that students who say they take notes in order to revise later on are merely using a conventional belief in order to rationalize an habitual and thoughtless activity, is well borne out by studies of students' use of their notes as revision tools. In a study carried out by Hartley and Cameron (1967) for example, while every single student said he intended to do follow-up work based on a particular set of notes, eighty-seven per cent of them did not even subsequently read those notes.

In their review on note taking, Howe and Godfrey (1978) suggest that the optimum procedure is *not* to take notes at the time of initial study, and to use a *handout*, a teacher-produced summary, as a revision tool, and that this results in better test scores than any other combination of activities.

I am *not* arguing here that we should advise students not to take notes: I am merely pointing out that what one might take to be an obvious piece of advice to give to students may be somewhat questionable. If we were to train our students to use a particular note taking technique we would almost certainly not be training them to do anything which is *necessary*, and our hopes that our students would become more efficient learners as a result would almost certainly not be supported by evidence. The same sort of problems arise if we examine any other aspect of studying than note taking. Many 'study habit inventories', paper and pencil tests of study skills, have been developed to test whether students are going about their studies in recommended ways. Such inventories typically contain items right across the range of learning activities on reading, organizing time and so on. Even the most extensive studies which have attempted to identify study habits that are associated with academic success have typically found only a very weak relationship between inventory scores and examination results, and seldom correlations even as large as + 0.1 (cf. Entwistle, 1977, Farrell, 1977). Furthermore, even if such correlations were greater they would *not* indicate a *causal* relationship between study habits and success. Many study habits are examples of the *consequence* of the way a student approaches studying, and cannot be taken to be *causes* of study success. For example, a diagnostic study habits inventory used by the University of Minnesota includes an item which asks students whether or not they sit at the front of the class. They also advise students to sit at the front. This is because they have found that students who sit at the front do better. This is obviously nonsense. Keen students sit at the front and keen students do better. Sitting a bored student at the front will not make any difference. Unfortunately practically all evidence concerning the consequences of study skills for learning is of this correlational nature. Edfeldt (1976) has argued that there is *no* evidence of *causal* relationships between observable study behaviour and learning outcomes.

It is vital at this point in the argument for us to recognize that this does *not* mean that all study techniques are useless. What it *does* mean is that if we generalize across all students and across all learning contexts, then we will not be able to detect any clear relationship between study techniques and learning outcomes. If we give advice in a *generalized* way, without regard to the individual student, or the particular course he is taking, (or the demands of its assessment system) then it is not very likely that we will have a positive effect. We do not, in general, know what the necessary study skills are, and it seems unlikely that any exist.

Is study skills advice rooted in sound experimental psychology or learning theory?

The advice or exercises one sees offered on study skills are often accompanied by implied, or even explicit, assumptions that it is all soundly based in the psychology of learning, scientific experimental work on memory, a fundamental understanding of the perceptual and cognitive processes involved in reading, and so on. *Use Your Head* the BBC book and TV series, which is widely used, the National Extension College's *How to Study Effectively* course studied by thousands of students, and most of the commercially available books and courses, claim scientific respectability in one way or another. Even when no such claim is made explicitly there is usually an implicit assumption that the advice offered could be justified on a sound experimental basis if needed. This is not just folk lore or common sense, the advice screams at the student 'it's *scientific* so how can you resist it?' Even when advice has managed to avoid such posturing I feel there is still the danger both that students will gain an over-inflated notion of the credentials of advice and that those giving the advice will be tempted to place more confidence in advice than is justified. I would like to question these apparent credentials and shake teachers' over-confidence by taking a close look at just one example of an area of advice that is given extremely widely but which has the most disreputable basis. The area I have chosen is that of advice on *learning and memory*. The supposed scientific basis for this advice may indeed be familiar to you as scholars in education and educational psychology − you may simply have never guessed that advice you were familiar with could possibly have been derived from such a basis. The inept way this area has been informed is an indictment of applied psychology, and also of the tendency for purveyors of advice to simply copy their wisdom from earlier purveyors of advice without ever questioning its basis.

Advice on memory and learning

Exposing the scientific basis of training in memory, and of study skills advice supposedly based on the psychology of learning, is like shooting fish in a barrel.

The forgetting curve

The main characteristic of memory, highlighted in advice (cf. Buzan 1973) is usually that things are forgotten very quickly indeed unless something is done about it. There is frequent reference to the dramatic and awe-inspiring forgetting curve (cf. Freeman, 1972).

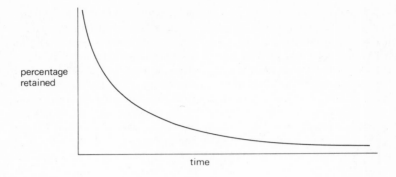

percentage retained

time

Graphs of the curve appear in all sorts of study skill books, usually displaying a bold disregard for labelling or graduating the axes or saying from whence the curve came. In fact it comes from Ebbinghaus (1885). He himself learnt long lists of nonsense syllables (e.g., FUJ, BEH, . . .) until he could remember them all. Then he waited for various lengths of time and saw how many times he had to go back through the list before he could remember them all again. His measure of retention was, therefore, how much effort had been saved in relearning the list. He found that after about twenty minutes he had to look through the list half as many times as he had done originally. This is interpreted by Buzan (1973) as meaning that fifty per cent of all learning is forgotten after twenty minutes. As any elementary educational psychology textbook will tell you there are some problems with such an interpretation:

1. The material Ebbinghaus used is absurdly unlike academic material. If you use meaningful material (e.g., lists of words or sentences) even within the other constraints of the experimental paradigm, the curve is *much* flatter, (e.g., Tyler, 1933). Obviously one remembers many things indefinitely.

2. The method of learning is absurdly unlike student learning. Going through and through a list may be all that one can do to memorize unconnected meaningless material. Students naturally adopt far more efficient strategies for learning meaningful material, unless advised otherwise. Clearly most things are 'memorized' in one trial, without any conscious effort. For example, do you remember your journey to this room this morning? Simply interacting in a meaningful way with the world results in a memory trace being formed. Our main problems are in *retrieving* such traces.

62

3. The method of testing memory is absurdly unlike student assessment. We do not put students through an examination again and again until they are word perfect and then see how long that took compared to such perfect mastery during the previous term. When people are asked to remember sentences, they remember the *meaning* without the surface *form*. For example you can probably remember the gist of how I opened this chapter without remembering the exact words I used. We make sense of our experience and automatically store in memory the sense we have made. If I tested you on your verbatim recall of the first sentences of this chapter you would score very poorly indeed, even if you had remembered the important things about it.

4. A good deal of the forgetting in the Ebbinghaus paradigm had been found, by the 1950s, to be due to 'interference' from the learning of other lists *prior* to the one tested, or *between* learning and recall of the one tested, rather than simply to passive decay of the memory trace. The more similar the interfering lists are, the more forgetting takes place. The learning of the crucial list is not *unique* enough to distinguish it in memory from memory traces of other lists of nonsense syllables. This is very unlike the learning situation facing students. If you were to test students on the exact form of words used in one of two different lectures on the same general topic, then presumably the similarity of the phrases habitually used would cause them problems in distinguishing one lecture from the other. But if you were to test them on their understanding of some concept or principle from one lecture then the similarity of conceptual framework from the other lecture would obviously *help* and not interfere.

Rehearsal

Clearly the forgetting curve is of extremely dubious relevance to student learning. This has not prevented Buzan (1973) and Main (1977), for example, from going on to give advice to students on the basis of what happens to this curve when you rehearse.

A graph is prepared, based rather loosely on Jost's law (1897). It is derived from exactly the same experimental paradigm as Ebbinghaus employed. Successively relearning the list of nonsense syllables results in successively shallower forgetting curves. It is concluded, in study skills advice, that to slow the relentless march of forgetting, you need to *rehearse* your material, at successively longer intervals. This must in-

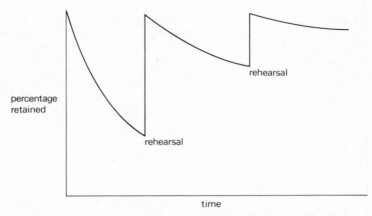

volve, says Buzan, rehearsing your notes immediately, after one day, one week, one month, etc. Apart from all the objections to the evidence for this phenomenon, outlined above, there are bizarre possibilities in store for any student who should follow such advice. A conventional student attending, say, four lectures a day and also taking notes from, say, two text sources a day, would, after only five weeks, be rehearsing 120 sets of notes a week! I have never met a student who would be willing to undertake such a task.

The learning plateau

The learning plateau is an established part of educational mythology and appears again and again in advice to students on how to study. For example:

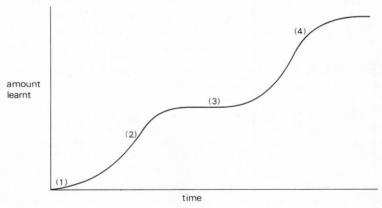

At stage (1), little progress is made because the subject is unfamiliar to the student. Then he enters stage (2), and makes rapid progress. After stage (2), during which he learnt quite a lot of material, he enters stage (3) — the plateau. Here he seems to be in the doldrums. Despite effort, no progress seems possible ... The plateau is the particular enemy of the home student who fails to realize that everyone reaches this sort of plateau. But if only they persevere they eventually move on to stage (4). At the end of stage (4), the student reaches his peak in this particular topic.

(Freeman, 1972, p. 19)

A student once explained to me that the reason why she was no longer getting anything out of her course text was that she was probably at the learning plateau she had been told to expect.

As usual with such advice, no source is provided. However, Maddox's *How to Study* cookbook (1963, p.51) at least describes an experiment on which it is based, and this turns out to be none other than the work of Book (1925). Book reports evidence of 174 consecutive daily half-hour practice sessions on a typewriter. In some individual cases there was, after about fifty days, a slight levelling off, for twenty days, of the daily increase in the number of correct typing strokes made during the session. In fact the learning plateau is a very unreliable and elusive phenomenon and tends to be tracked down only during similarly drawn out practice with simple motor skills. Its relevance to conceptual learning is therefore rather limited!

A danger with such pseudo-scientific 'explanations' of phenomena experienced by students is that they encourage a passive approach towards learning. Buffeted this way and that by apparently inexorable laws of learning the poor student must feel helpless in the face of study problems.

The sort of criticism I have made here, of the inadequacy of the empirical basis of some of the advice on memory and learning, can also be made of advice on many other study skills, especially of advice on fast reading. I would not like to give the impression that *all* the most commonly given study skills advice has no reputable basis whatsoever. However, its basis is often a good deal less sound than books and courses suggest.

What happens when you tell people how to learn?

Despite all the objections and problems which have been raised so far we may sometimes still have the feeling that we know exactly what it is that a particular student ought to be doing if he or she is to learn more effectively. However, even if we have correctly diagnosed a need for a *necessary* study skill and we have a *valid* analysis of what that skill consists of in order to be able to give the advice, we are still likely to have a very great deal of difficulty getting the student to adopt the skill. Both giving advice and training through exercises, involve many problems.

Some advice, though based on a sound understanding of what the end product of studying looks like is impossible to take because it lacks an understanding of the process by which this product is achieved. Advice on how to concentrate, for example, may include a reasonable description of the state of mind when one is concentrating, but be completely unhelpful as to how to achieve it. People simply cannot concentrate 'at will', it is a state reached as a *by-product* of being engaged in, or absorbed by, a task.

Some advice is impossible to take because what is described is impossible. The advice, on writing sentences, that one should first think through to the end of the sentence before starting to write it is simply impossible to follow even for experienced proficient writers, (Britton, 1975). On the other hand some advice is impossible, or disruptive, to follow for particular people. This may be partly due to the variation between learners, and partly due to the weakness of the understanding of studying on which the advice is based. A good example is advice on planning written work before undertaking it. It is almost universal to advise students to produce a plan for an essay before they write it. James Britton (1975) has studied the development of writing abilities in secondary school children and found that their ways of planning, and their attitudes towards planning, varied very widely:

> Before any big essay, for example, in English Literature, I think to myself 'Yes, plan an essay like Miss . . . said' but I begin to plan it and then suddenly the urge to start the actual piece of written work is over-powering − and 'bang' goes the plan . . . I can rely on this happening every time without exception.

> I cannot bear writing to a plan. I can rarely be induced to write my own, and the thought of writing to someone else's plan fills me with horror . . . It has just occurred to me that when writing literature essays I always scribble down all clever thoughts on paper first. Then sometimes I may even write a complete rough essay but usually I write the final essay, using the written facts as a guide to help me think out the argument. I do not know if 'clever thoughts' rate as a plan . . .

> Earlier this year when I was revising . . . I learnt that I write better without a plan. If I just pour my thoughts out on paper I build up a

type of plan anyway. But if I try to jot down notes my mind just goes blank.

The problem here seems to be the way students perceive planning. The real planning many people do is often so informal and messy as to pass unrecognized. Clearly the lack of any planning at all can be disastrous, but very formal planning can also be disruptive and unhelpful. When advice over-formalizes what is normally an informal process it can become impossible to follow. For example, the reading method SQ3R (Survey, Question, Read, Recall, Review), which is described in many study manuals, is meant to loosen up reading and to free readers from rigid unadoptive habits. But the comments of some students suggest that it may itself be understood as an inflexible set of rules and seen as a tedious and irrelevant route to have to take. In other cases the very communication of the message may embody such contradictions. A model of 'flexible reading' presented in one manual (Open University, 1979, p.27) uses an algorithm to convey its message. One might argue, however, that this algorithm presents an appearance of inflexibility. For example: 'Is the book a collection of articles?' 'Yes'. 'Preview: rapid skimming of whole book, establishing content, structure, tone. Do you intend to read on?' 'No'. 'Is the book only useful in certain parts?' etc. There would appear to be a conflict here between the intention of the advice and the effect it would be likely to have if it were followed.

Some advice does not lead to any change, even when it has been accepted by students. There are several ways this seems to happen, and they all emphasize some aspect of the difference between knowing how to do something and actually doing it. Students often have rationalizations for their study habits which bear little relationship to what they actually do. As I have already mentioned, students often claim that the reason they take notes is to revise from them afterwards — but they *do not* often revise from them because this can be such a dull and profitless activity. While attempting to teach students how to study through a National Extension College course (Freeman, 1972) my students were required to send me their notes from a chapter of the course text which covered note taking. A good proportion of these students had copied out, word for word, the advice in the text always to take notes in one's own words! Also, some had copied advice to structure notes in one's own way and use one's own headings, and had embedded this advice in notes laid out, structured, and headed, *exactly* as in the chapter. Clearly these students had learnt the advice, at some level, without it influencing their studying in any way. Sometimes students are well aware of the gap between what they 'ought' to be doing, and what they know they are doing. These mature students I interviewed in 1975 seemed to have a growing awareness of the advice they were being given by their tutors, and were also aware that they were not doing what they were expected to, even though they would have liked to:

JILL: Mike's comments have told me why my essays aren't proper essays but though I know what I should be doing I still can't write them. He says 'you haven't discussed this, you haven't clarified this, you've taken lots of ideas from people and repeated them and made conclusions' and I know what I *should* be doing but I'm still not doing it.

INTERVIEWER: Why do you think you can't learn from this advice?

JILL: Well, I don't know how to put ideas together yet. We should have learnt that from our class discussions but we don't seem to have. Our class discussions should help us bring ideas together and formulate them.

DEE: And what we tend to do is just to regurgitate what we've read before.

BARBARA: This is what Marjorie has been trying to do with us from the start, and I don't think we've really appreciated that − last week she was saying 'But what do *you* think?'

SHEILA: Yes, she wanted *your* thoughts.

DEE: But that's the first time I've felt it come across . . .

BARBARA: I've known what she wanted, but I haven't been able to do it.

Sometimes the gap between knowing and doing is evident in the lack of *transfer* of approaches to studying from one domain to another. This is sometimes wrongly taken to indicate that the student lacks some ability altogether. For example, that a schoolchild cannot ever remember his French vocabulary is taken to indicate that he has a poor memory, though he will no doubt remember who scored the goals in the Cup Final. A study skills course may try and teach students how to be evaluative in essays, when they are perfectly capable of being evaluative in other aspects of their lives: in choosing a boyfriend or deciding whether the manager of the England football team is any good. This lack of transfer is sometimes evident in a very stark way even within one piece of work. One of my National Extension College students had submitted an assignment to me in which she was asked to exercise her powers of critical thinking on some *Daily Telegraph* articles. She had carried out a superb job of demolition on the arguments, pointing out misuse of evidence, appeals to authority, emotive language, and so on. Having completed this impressive task she could not resist offering her own opinion on the topic of the articles and proceeded to commit every logical fault she had just, correctly, accused the articles of committing!

Evidence for the effectiveness of study skill courses is extremely thin on the ground. While it is relatively easy to get students to perform all sorts of clever tricks during courses, it is much harder to transfer significant changes over to everyday studying. In fact evidence is somewhat damning. Gadzella *et al.* (1977) found no difference in academic performance between those who had received guidance and a carefully chosen control group of similar students and Reid (1977) found only *short-term* differences in study habits and even a deterioration in some habits, as a consequence of one of the most highly developed and heavily-sold courses in Britain.

Finally, students sometimes do not follow advice, even though they value it, because it involves a threatening attack on their existing ways of doing things. Even the most confident of us would hesitate at the thought of making a complete twenty-four hour timetable of our work for the next week. We *know* that it would help us see how much we were getting done and help us to plan our tasks, but the thought of being confronted with all the unreconcilable demands and writing down every evening: 'watched TV'; is just too horrible, so we do not do it. I have had students who *know* that the way they take notes is ridiculous and useless, but who lack the confidence to abandon their note taking technique for another which they *know* will be more useful. In my experience, the less happy and secure a student is in his existing habits, the less likely he is to abandon them in the hope that some new technique will improve things. Simply knowing the advice is not enough.

I believe that quite often students do not follow advice simply because what is suggested sounds so unappealing. The model of a super-efficient, hard-working, well-organized, conscientious student embodied in much advice is a pretty off-putting one to those of us who like to feel that learning has more to do with imagination and creativeness and who recognize that learning plays only a limited part along with many other aspects of our lives. There are limits to what I am willing to do in order to become more efficient. I may be frequently missing deadlines but I am not willing to timetable myself any more rigidly. Working late at night may be less efficient than early in the morning, but I cannot face working early in the morning. We often seem to ask of students things we are not willing to do, or even try, ourselves. It is not very surprising when they do not do what we ask.

One way of overcoming these problems with the giving of advice is to go one step further and *train* students to use whatever methods of study you happen to prefer. There are also problems with training. The first thing that happens when you train someone to do something new is that they get worse at it. In almost any area of training, changing technique initially results in *worse* performance. A new reading technique will take you longer, a new way of writing essays will exhaust you, a new way of taking notes will result in you writing down a lot of nonsense. In time, with practice and support, you may well get better, much better than with the old technique. But the first experience is usually one of unfamiliarity, confusion, slowness and self-consciousness. New techniques temporarily disrupt studying. Without support, encouragement, and the opportunity to practise in contexts which do not matter too much, it is very likely that any new technique will be dropped at this early stage, before it starts being helpful.

However, a student's problems are not over if he has got past this point and actually adopted the new technique. Being trained may not always be a good thing unless the training also involves some help as to how to use the skill *appropriately* and with *purpose*. Most study techniques embody assumptions about the purposes of the technique, or the purposes of studying in general. The student may well not be aware of these assumptions, may misunderstand them, or may not share them and not realize any incompatibility. This may have unfortunate consequences. Students attending study skill training programmes often seem to trustingly abandon all responsibility toward the purpose of the tasks in which they employ the technique. For example, William Perry (1959), as cited in Chapter 2, describes what happened when 800 Harvard students with superb fast reading skills tackled a chapter of a book, and were stopped after twenty minutes:

> We can report that their rate of work in this particular approach was astonishing and their capacity to answer multiple-choice questions on detail was impressive. Some of them had read as many as twenty pages of very detailed material and were able to answer accurately every sensible question we could ask them about the detail . . . We asked anyone who could do so to write a short statement about what the chapter was all about. The number who were able to tell us . . . was just one in a hundred-fifteen.

In other words ninety-nine per cent of these skilled readers were going about reading this chapter in a way which did not involve an attempt to find out what it was about. Perry described their efforts as 'obedient purposelessness' and went on to conclude:

> Until such students revise their sense of the purpose of reading, an increase in effort is likely to produce only worse results.

. . . the mechanics of reading skill are inseparable at this level from the individual's purpose as he reads. If you train someone in mechanics alone, he drops right back into his old habits the minute he picks up an assigned text.

This sorry state of affairs cannot be remedied simply by giving advice. As one of Perry's students who had discovered that he had just approached his reading in an inappropriate way remarked: 'Oh Lord, how many times have I been told!' Training in fast reading is particularly prone to misorientation. Worse still, Perry found that a third of the students who were misoriented in their reading also appeared to be oriented towards the wrong goals in their writing. The crucial importance of *orientation* and *purpose* should be noted here and will be picked up again in the next section.

It seems to have been an unquestioned assumption of educational technology that one can diagnose the absence of crucial learning 'skills' and cure this by training students in these skills. I hope this section has made it clear that this is a questionable assumption. I do not want to claim that all 'study skills' advice, and all attempts at training students to use techniques, are absolute nonsense. But I hope I have made it clear that considerable, and sometimes overwhelming, problems face attempts to give advice and train students in a generalized way. At the right time, in the right context, both advice and training have their place, but as servants of other approaches, and not as ends in themselves.

CHAPTER 5

In what ways do students develop as learners?

If diagnosing students' learning ills in terms of their lack of general learning *skills* brings with it a multitude of problems, how else are we to approach helping students? If it is not primarily learning *skills* that they lack, how are we to understand why students sometimes do not learn effectively? In this section I will examine the nature of differences between the ways people learn, and, in particular, examine how people develop and change as they become more sophisticated learners. If we can understand what underlies this development we will be in a better position to foster it.

Students do not simply study in the way they do because they only know how to use certain study techniques. Students actively *choose* to study in the way they do.

Nor can their studying be understood simply in terms of fixed personal characteristics such as learning style (e.g., field-dependence/ independence or serialist/holist). I have argued elsewhere why learning style explanations are, by themselves, inadequate (Gibbs, Morgan and Taylor, 1980).

There are many studies in which students have been shown to give reasons for the way they study. In studies by Becker *et al.* (1968) and Snyder (1971) in American universities there are vivid examples of students talking about their studying, and why they believe they work in the way they do. Similar students in the context of British universities (e.g., Parlett *et al.* 1976) also describe students as definers of their own study tasks. It might be argued that such student explanations are merely *post hoc* rationalizations for behaviour which is determined by the students' limited skills or fixed learning styles. However two recent longitudinal studies in British universities would seem to overcome this objection, as they trace *changes* in students' explanations over the course of their studies.

Beaty, (1978) in order to understand students' study habits and use of the library, interviewed students over the full three years of their course, about *why* they were studying. She developed the notion of the 'study contract' which students implicitly make as a sort of statement of aims and ways of achieving those aims while at university.

> ... students come to University with ideas of what it will be like and with aims of various stages of development. Through interaction with others and experience of the University and course they develop a study strategy, tentative at first, which is consistent with their aims and self-identity. This organisation of attitudes and study patterns soon affects educational outcomes in the form of essay marks, but also in knowledge gained, etc. This provides the student with object-ive and subjective feedback on the effectiveness of their strategy and allows them to reinterpret and perhaps re-design the Study Contract by changing strategy or perhaps aims in order to be consistent once more.

Beaty showed second year students the transcripts of their first year interview and they recognized the sentiments they had expressed a year before and were able to explain how things had changed and how they now saw things differently. This active reassessment and changing of study strategy over time is also illustrated in a study by Mathias (1978). He identified two general 'types' of approaches to learning: 'course-focus' and 'interest-focus'. Course-focused students stuck to the syllabus (rather in the manner of Hudson's 'syllabus-bound' behaviour) e.g., 'if you do things which are not on the syllabus they're not going to come up in the exams. The only thing you really come to University for is to get a degree.' In contrast, an 'interest-focused' student said 'If I were really interested I would try to read more about it and possibly go and see the tutor again depending on how deeply interested I was.' Mathias points out that there can be no simple explanation for this differences:

> These behaviours did not represent static mental characteristics of students fixed in time, but rather could vary over time as the student moved through his degree course. It seemed more likely that a com-bination of factors were at work whose interaction and behavioural product was mediated through some process of interpretation on the part of the student.

For example, some students in Mathias' study started off with a weak course-focus but over the three years of their course changed their orientation to a strong course-focus:

> Over the first year they comfortably coped with the degree course, seemed able to work with little support and showed a high level of interest in their chosen subjects in which they were willing to place extra effort. They sought a high level of interaction and stimulation from their tutors in order to engage their interests. However during the second year they reassessed their attitude to University and began to question their high level of commitment to their study. This reassessment seemed to come about through a growing self-awareness of the relationship between themselves, University study, and other interests and activities University had to offer. They carried into University a style of work developed at school which was characterized by a high level of commitment. At the same time they also had high expectations of intellectual stimulation. However, they were somewhat disappointed with the level of intellectual stimulation they encountered on their course . . . By the third year they were less likely to emphasise their own interests . . .

A 'strong course-focus' has implications not simply for the *amount* of work students put in or the *degree* of commitment, but *what* is studied and *how*. Study methods are adopted and used in ways which are intended to achieve particular goals and it makes little sense to talk about study methods without reference to the use to which they may be put by students. The range of general orientations students have when they join university is poorly understood at present. Furthermore students may initially be unclear or unrealistic about their orientation. The development of approaches to learning parallels the development of awareness of orientation and of the appropriateness of particular study methods for particular orientations.

Not only do students have different general orientations to study, but they understand the demands of specific learning tasks in different ways. And, as with orientations, this understanding develops and changes over time. I will described two complementary frameworks which are currently available to help us to understand the nature of these developments. In both these frameworks the focus of attention is not on the acquisition of study skills, but on the development of increasingly sophisticated conceptions of what learning involves. Students come to understand progressively more about studying. There are many clues that this is so from studies in British contexts. For example Miller and Parlett (1974) have found that some students were much more aware than others of the demands of the learning context. They found almost half the students in their study to be 'cue-deaf' —

that is they were oblivious to cues about exactly what was to be learned. In both the Beaty and Mathias studies referred to above there are numerous suggestions that students become more aware, and more able to consciously choose personally relevant learning strategies, as they become more experienced learners.

The first framework I shall describe is one outcome of an extensive study at Göteborg University entitled 'Study Skill and Learning'. The background to the aspect I shall describe is that some students were demonstrated to have achieved exceptionally poor understanding from reading articles and indeed from taking entire courses. In one study (Dahlgren, 1979a) some university students' understanding of fundamental economics principles was no better after an economics course than before. Indeed in some cases it was actually worse. What is more, some conceptions held by these students were not in any important way different from those held by second grade schoolchildren (Dahlgren, 1979b). How was it that these students could understand so little as a consequence of a university course? What were these students doing in their studying?

In both experimental studies, and in the context of everyday studying, the ways students experience studying has been examined by the Göteborg group. In experimental studies (e.g., Marton and Säljö, 1976a) students have been asked to introspect about their experience of reading a text. It has emerged that students' descriptions are of only *two* rather different sorts. In one sort, students described their approach in the following way:

Well, I just concentrated on trying to remember as much as possible.

I remembered . . . but, I'd sort of memorized everything I'd read . . . no, not everything, but more or less.

It would have been more interesting if I'd known that I wasn't going to be tested on it afterwards, 'cos in that case I'd've more, you know, thought about what it said instead of all the time trying to think now I must remember this and now I must remember that.

In the other sort of description, students said:

. . . I tried to look for . . . you know, the principal ideas . . .

. . . and what you think about then, well it's you know, what was the point of the article, you know . . .

No, I . . . tried to think what it was all about . . .

... I thought about how he had built up the whole thing.

This sort of difference of approach they have repeatedly encountered in different studies, and it has also been clearly evident in two studies in British universities (Laurillard, 1979, at Surrey; and Ramsden, 1979, at Lancaster). I am convinced that many university students, even experienced students, consistently adopt the first approach described above.

It is important to note that this is not simply a quantitative difference in a variable such as motivation or attention. It is a *qualitative* difference of level of approach. In the first sort of description students have the discourse itself, the sign, as a focus of attention, and in the second sort of description students were concerned with what the discourse was about — what was signified. These two categories of approach have been labelled 'surface approach' and 'deep approach' respectively.

But to what extent are these descriptions of level of approach a fixed characteristic of the students? It has been a common practice in quantitative studies of the approaches students take to their studies (for example, Witkin's studies of field-dependence/independence, e.g., Witkin *et al.* 1977) to look for consistencies among students' behaviour and to attribute these to some notion of cognitive style or learning style which is relatively unchanging from situation to situation, rather like a personality characteristic. Is the surface/deep distinction of this nature?

Well, some evidence of consistency certainly exists. For example, Svensson (1977) found that twenty-three of the thirty students in his study took the same approach in his experimental studies as they did in their normal studies. This sort of evidence has been used to develop a questionnaire which is intended to identify 'surface processors' and 'deep processors'. However, if one looks at learning in *specific* contexts, and *asks* students, one gets a rather different picture of the nature of the surface/deep distinction.

First, Diana Laurillard, at Surrey University, has shown that students will take a surface or deep approach to a task *depending on the nature of the task*. She required students to teach back to her material which they were studying on their science course. The variation in students' approaches became apparent when the specific content and context of the learning were examined (Laurillard, 1979). Students adopted a surface approach to some tasks, and a deep approach to others.

Second, Roger Säljö (1979c) introduced the notions of surface and deep approach to seventy-two subjects, by asking them to read a paper about this in an experiment:

... a clear majority of subjects participating in this study recognise the dichotomy between a deep and surface approach and they can furthermore relate their own methods and procedures of learning to this perspective. A surprising result, however, is the finding that very few describe themselves as belonging exclusively to either of these categories. Rather, the general attitude among 61 out of the 72 subjects, who described their own learning in the perspective outlined in the text used as learning material, is that they consider both of these approaches to be applicable to their own learning . . . the subjects perceive their approach to learning as being contextually dependent.

For these students we would need to look at the way specific learning contexts were conceptualized and experienced by the students in order to understand why a surface approach is sometimes adopted.

However, there were also a number of students in Säljö's study who:

. . . adopt a surface approach to learning because they have a conception which does not make it possible for them to go about learning in any other way. Their inability to understand the distinction between a deep and a surface approach may in fact be a sign of just this.

So while for some there was an awareness of contextual influences, and even the possibility of choice about which approach to learning to adopt, for others:

There may not be any room for such contextual influences simply because learning is held to have one fairly obvious meaning which does not differ from one situation to another.

For these students we would need to look at their *conception of learning* in order to understand why a surface approach is always adopted. I shall go on to look at the distinctions different students are able to make about the demands of specific learning. But first I should like to emphasize why it is so important to understand *why* students sometimes adopt a surface approach.

The Göteborg group have clearly demonstrated a relationship between the approach a student takes to a learning task and the learning outcome, between students' descriptions of their own approach on the one hand and the quality of the content of their learning on the other. For example in one study (Marton and Säljö, 1976a) students were asked to read an article concerning curriculum reform in the Swedish universities. They were then asked 'Try to summarize the article in one or two sentences. What is the author trying to say, in other words?' In the article the author argued that a blanket approach to reform aimed at raising pass rates was misguided, and that *selective* measures should be taken which concentrated on particular categories of students.

It was found that *students'* answers fell into four categories:

A. Selective measures were to be taken, i.e., *only* for particular categories of students.
B. Different measures were to be taken for different groups.
C. Measures were to be taken.
D. There are differences between groups.

These students were also asked to introspect concerning the way they had gone about reading the article, and their comments were categorized in terms of the distinction described above, i.e., surface approach/deep approach. The relationship between the approach students took and what they learned can be seen in Table 1.

Table 1   Relationship between approach and outcome

Level of approach	Level of outcome			
	A	B	C	D
Surface	0	1	8	5
Not clear	0	6	0	1
Deep	5	4	0	0

It is clear that the approach students took to reading was very important. None of the students who described their approach in terms categorized as a surface level approach completely understood the author's argument, while none of the students who took a deep approach failed to gain a good understanding. This sort of clear-cut relationship has been demonstrated again and again. Students who adopt a surface approach understand less.

Further work at Göteborg (Svensson, 1976, 1977) has shown that this relationship exists in everyday studies as well as in experiments. In an experiment he found students adopted one of two different approaches. Students who adopted what he calls an 'atomistic' approach focused on specific comparisons in a text, focused on the parts in sequence, on memorizing details, and lacked an orientation towards the message as a whole. In contrast, students who adopted what he calls a 'holistic' approach focused on understanding the overall meaning of the text, searched for the author's intention etc. (These categories are clearly similar to the surface/deep distinction, as well as to distinctions drawn by Bruner, and by Pask, on the basis of rather different evidence.)

Students were categorized according to which approach they described themselves as adopting, and also according to whether their recall of the text contained a conclusion or not. Combining delayed recall data from students and study of two texts, a clear relationship between students' approach and their learning outcome was again found (see Table 2).

Table 2 Relationship between approach and outcome for delayed recall of two texts

Approach	Outcome	
	Conclusion	No conclusion
Holistic	22	0
Atomistic	12	25

Abridged from Table 2, Svensson, 1977

These students were closely followed over a year of their normal studies on a course. Their approach to their everyday studies was investigated, and it was found that 23 out of 30 studied in the same way as in the experiment. Of these 23, 10 were categorized as adopting a holistic approach in both experimental and normal studies and 13 were categorized as adopting an atomistic approach in both studies. Of the 10 adopting a holistic approach, 9 passed the course. Of the 13 adopting an atomistic approach, only 3 passed the course. Again, despite the small numbers in the study (enforced by the methodology employed) there were very clear-cut results. It is important to notice that such clear-cut results are in marked contrast to the very weak relationships that have been found between study skills inventory scores and performance.

Svensson also examined the relationship between the numbers of hours students spent per week, whether they revised for the examination, and what sort of study techniques they used. By making four dichotomous decisions about each student (holist/atomist; greater or less than three hours study a week; revised/did not revise; elaborated or restricted study technique) he was able to predict correctly the exam outcome of twenty-nine of the thirty students in the study. However, unlike those advocating a 'study skills' explanation of such findings, he understands the relative diligence and study techniques of students *in relation to their approach*, not as isolated, technical skills. Adopting an atomistic approach brings with it problems — study becomes boring and revision is very hard to undertake in a productive way. And in fact for those adopting an atomistic approach, time commitment tailed off as the course progressed. The approach one adopts has *consequences* for study techniques. As I pointed out earlier, variation in technique alone accounts for *very* little variation in learning outcome. Study techniques are thus seen as having *functional relationships* with students' approach. There is further support for these conclusions in similar studies elsewhere (e.g. Goldman, 1972; Biggs, 1976).

> . . . to sum up it would appear that a decisive factor in non-verbatim learning, both in experimental settings and in everyday work, is the learner's approach to learning.
>
> (Marton, 1975)

What is it that underlies a student's approach to learning? One member of the research group at Göteborg, Roger Säljö, has concerned himself with this question, and with the differences between students. In particular he has attempted to describe the different ways in which students conceptualize learning. When he asked ninety people (Säljö, 1978, 1979b) of as wide a variety as possible, about their conceptions of learning, he discovered that for some the phenomenon of learning in itself had become an object of reflection, whereas for others it had not. For some, learning was something which could be explicitly talked about, discussed, consciously planned, and analysed. For others, it was taken for granted. He found that students take three main 'steps' in the development of their reflection about learning. They make the following three distinctions:

1. The first of these distinctions concerns subjects reporting themselves *as becoming aware of the influence of the context in learning about what you should learn and how you should set about it.* Thus, subjects report that at some time or another they started to try to adapt their learning to various kinds of demands (e.g. teachers, tests, etc). This is of course the perspective described by, for instance, Snyder (1971) and Miller and Parlett (1974) and, to follow the terminology suggested by the last two researchers, this distinction implies that subjects somehow become 'cue-conscious', i.e. they become aware of the implicit rules governing learning in a school context. Whether or not subjects decide to adapt their learning to these rules is a different problem. The main thing is, however, that they become aware of such demands.

2. The two remaining distinctions are more closely linked to the activity of learning as such. The first of these refers to a distinction between *learning 'for life' versus learning in school.* Quite a large proportion of the subjects make this distinction, the essen-

tial nature of which seems to be that learning in school is perceived of as an activity which, to a too large extent, has become stereotyped and routine, guided only by the needs and principles of schools themselves. Learning in school is thus held to be a particular activity whose prime feature is artificiality in the sense that it is not perceived of as being organically related to anything outside the school situation. Many of the subjects who analyse learning in school on the basis of this distinction are consequently very negative and critical. However, for our present purposes it may suffice to say that the discovery of this problematic nature of learning in educational contexts seems to many to serve as a step through which learning becomes thematized.

3. Perhaps the most interesting distinction in the present data concerns the fact that at certain points subjects report themselves as having started to think about the nature of what is learned or, following the terminology of Colaizzi (1973), the nature of the learned content. This distinction is introduced by the subjects themselves as that between either *learning and real learning*, or even more commonly, as that between *learning and understanding*.

   Real learning or understanding is, in this case, contrasted with rote learning and its main feature is considered to be that it in some way involves the abstraction of meaning (cf. Colaizzi, 1973) from learning materials rather than a mere reproduction of them. In a sense, the nature of what is learned is perceived of to be more complex and to have a more holistic nature; it is a perspective, a point of view, an interpretation, a principle, etc, rather than the plain 'facts' which subjects previously report themselves as having perceived of as what is to be learned. These facts are now seen instead as subordinated to what should really be learned, i.e. the general meaning.

Säljö (1979a) has also studied people's conceptions of learning directly by simply asking them 'What do you actually mean by learning?' Their answers revealed five rather different conceptions: (these are extracts from pages 12–19).

Conception 1: Learning as the increase of knowledge
The main feature of this first category is its vagueness in the sense that what is given in the answers is merely a set of synonyms for the word learning.
S: . . . it's to increase your knowledge . . .
E: . . . hum . . . could you stay something further?
S: . . . well, you kind of start with a small bag and there is not much in it, but then the longer you live, the more you fill it up . . .

Conception 2: Learning as memorizing

. . . The meaning of learning is to transfer units of information or pieces of knowledge, or what is commonly referred to simply as facts, from an external source, such as a teacher or a book, into the head.

S: To learn . . . well as I understand the word . . . sort of to listen and to get inside . . . acquire knowledge kind of . . . yes, quite simply to learn it . . . yes sort of to learn, to get things in one's head so they stay there.

Conception 3: Learning as the acquisition of facts, procedures, etc., which can be retained and/or utilized in practice.

Compared to the previous conceptions . . . some facts, principles etc. are considered to be practically useful and/or possible to remember for a long period of time, and as a consequence of this they should be learned.

S: Yes to learn so that you know it and so that you can make use of it. It shouldn't be just learning something which disappears immediately after you've learned it, but you should be able to make use of it even after a while . . .

Conception 4: Learning as the abstraction of meaning

Compared to the previous two categories the distinctive characteristic of this conception is that the nature of what is learned is changed. Learning is no longer conceived of as an activity of reproduction, but instead as a process of abstracting meaning from what you read and hear.

S: For me, personally, learning does not mean that you should learn all those petty details, but instead it means learning about a course of events and how things have developed, and reasoning within my subject but it does not mean sitting and memorizing trifles such as dates and such things as people do . . .

. . . the reproductive nature of learning is replaced by a conception which emphasizes that learning is a constructive activity. The learning material is not seen as containing ready-made knowledge to be memorized, but rather it provides the raw material or starting-point for learning.

Conception 5: Learning as an interpretative process aimed at the understanding of reality.

This conception of learning is very similar to the previous one in the sense that the picture which is supplied in the descriptions concerning the nature of what is learning is very much the same. The reason for making a further distinction is that some subjects emphasize that an essential element of learning is that what you learn should help you interpret the reality in which you live.

S: Yes, learning that means to get a sort of insight into your subject so that you can use it in your everyday life. In some ways I think I've found out that you learn things twice somehow. The first time could have been at school really, the second time is the connection, I mean it becomes conscious in some way . . . I mean it should be related to some kind of practice. That's when you have learnt it, I think, terribly much. Then you can live . . . I mean you can sort of *be* your knowledge in some way. Then, the really important thing has happened . . .

Säljö highlights fundamental differences underlying these conceptions:

> A prominent feature of especially the second conception described above is the idea that knowledge is external to individuals and that the process of learning essentially means a more or less verbatim item-by-item transfer of knowledge from an external source, into the heads of the learners where it is filed. In contrast the essence of conceptions 4 and 5 seems to lie very much in an emphasis on the assumption that knowledge is construed by individuals as a result of an active effort on the part of the learner to abstract meaning from a discourse and also to relate this meaning to an outside reality.

It also seems that the qualitative differences between conceptions 2 and 3 on the one hand, and 4 and 5 on the other, are very similar to the distinction between surface and deep level approaches to learning identified in experimental studies. It seeems likely that the approach people adopt to learning tasks has to do with their conception of what knowledge and learning are (a similar point to that emphasized by Perry (1970)).

Those students Säljö identified who held learning 'to have one fairly obvious meaning which does not differ from one situation to another' are likely (i) not to have yet made the distinctions outlined above and (ii) to hold a conception of learning nearer to conception 1 than to conception 5. Referring back to the economics study mentioned earlier, many of the students whose understanding of economics concepts did not change over the course are likely to have adopted a surface approach to studying. That some of these students may have done this may be understood in terms of the conceptions of learning held by these students. What is crucial to the development of students as learners is that new study skills are seldom learnt and employed to any useful end without first facilitating the development of students' conception of learning. I believe this to be true on the basis of a good deal of personal experience counselling individual students about their study methods. Without first exploring and discussing what it is the student is aiming to achieve by taking notes/reading/writing an essay/revising or whatever, my suggestions concerning *techniques* have usually been utterly futile. And by and large, unless I can somehow bring about a reconceptualization of the nature of the exercise that they are involved in in studying, then the scope for my bringing about any useful change in their studying is extremely limited. When I *have* been able to bring about such a reconceptualization, the scope for the adoption of new techniques (in an appropriate way) has been dramatic and exciting.

A second framework for conceptualizing the way students change is offered by Perry (1979). For twenty years Perry ran the Bureau of Study Counsel at Harvard University. Initially running study skill courses, he moved towards individual study counselling based around an understanding of students' stage of development. This understanding is based on an extensive and prolonged interview study of Harvard students. Here Perry illustrates his 'scheme of intellectual development' with a brief example:

> Let us suppose that a lecturer announces that today he will consider three theories explanatory of – (whatever his topic may be). Student A has always taken it for granted that knowledge consists of correct answers, that there is one right answer per problem, and that teachers explain these answers for students to learn. He therefore listens for the lecturer to state which theory he is to learn.
>
> Student B makes the same general assumptions but with an elaboration to the effect that teachers sometimes present problems and procedures, rather than answers 'so that we can learn to find the right answer on our own'. He therefore perceives the lecture as a kind of guessing game in which he is to 'figure out' which theory is correct . . .
>
> Student C assumes that an answer can be called 'right' only in the light of its context, and that contexts, or 'frames of reference' differ. He assumes that several interpretations of a poem, explanations of a historical development, or even theories of a class of events in physics, may be legitimate 'depending on how you look at it'. – He supposes that the lecturer may be about to present three legitimate theories which can be examined for their internal coherence, their scope, their fit with various data, their predictive power etc.
>
> Whatever the lecturer then proceeds to do . . . these three students will make meaning of the experience in different ways . . .
>
> (Perry, 1970)

Perry in fact described *nine* stages of development through which students progress from an extreme absolutist position, through relativism to a flexible commitment, but the three, labelled A, B and C in the example quoted here, indicate the broad variation to be found. What students understand to be demanded of them in a learning situation will be dependent on the limits of their intellectual development and so delimit how they will tackle learning tasks. This is not simply an esoteric scheme, it is easily applicable. For example, while researching at the Open University, interviewing students studying the Foundation School Science course, D101, I encountered a clear example of a 'B' type student. This student had taken Technology courses to fill his degree profile, and was taking D101, as his second Foundation course requirement, as his *last* course before graduating. His Technology courses had evidently not disturbed his fundamental absolutism. He recognized that D101 was examining, for example, a variety of possible explanations of crime, but complained bitterly that in the end the course did not tell him what the cause of crime was. An absolutist stance such as this is disastrous for a social science student and completely overrides any significance the study techniques he adopted might have had. It determined *what* he wrote in his notes, for example, regardless of his note-taking technique.

In Perry's study he reported transcripts of interviews with students which demonstrated that students become increasingly aware of the epistemological stance they have adopted, and even aware of the next step they must take and of the disturbing consequences for the coherence of their ideas which such a step must inevitably involve. I have encountered one such student in the same D101 study mentioned above. This student explained that he had always taken a critical and relativistic approach to TV documentaries, serious newspaper articles and so on, but had held Open University material in awe and had simply 'learnt' all the explanations of the causes of crime in D101 without any distinction. They were all equally correct in his eyes. One had no way of choosing. However, during the summer school he had had to play the role of juror in a simulated rape trial, and in order to decide on the guilt of the accused he had had to come off his totally relativist fence and move towards some commitment to one explanation rather than another. He had recognized the significance of this change of stance and described to me how his approach to the course material would change as a consequence. Details of his general study habits remained quite unchanged and were by and large irrelevant to what he actually did with the ideas in the course.

Perry's study counselling has been centrally concerned with students' intellectual and ethical development rather than with study techniques. In his time at Harvard he has seen the intellectual stage at which students enter Harvard become more advanced — a phenomenon he attributes to increasingly relativistic teaching in schools and decreasingly authoritative presentation of knowledge and teaching methods.

I think there is a tendency to believe that to reorient students and to get them to adopt study techniques with *purpose*, all one has to do is mention purpose in passing, or simply tell students what purpose they must adopt. I hope the above has made it clear that students' orientation and understanding of purpose are *deep-rooted*, fundamental aspects of their approach to learning tasks, which *change slowly* and with difficulty, and which can bring about disorienting consequences when they do develop and change. They are also not simply 'important things to bear in mind' but *prerequisites* for development. As I earlier quoted Perry (1959) as stating: 'Until . . . students revise their sense of purpose . . . an increase in effort is likely to produce only worse results.' And students need to develop a more sophisticated conception of learning or a more sophisticated epistemological stance in order to revise their sense of purpose.

CHAPTER 6

How can students' development be facilitated?

The practical strategies for teaching students to learn which I advocate in this book can be deduced partially from the previous two sections. I believe that telling students how to learn is not often justifiable or effective, and I believe that developments in students' fundamental conceptions of learning underlie developments in their practical studying behaviour. But linking these two beliefs and providing a rationale for my strategies is a broader set of beliefs concerning how people develop and change, how they learn *at all*, rather than beliefs specifically concerned with studying. These beliefs are based largely in *constructivist* notions (e.g., the personal construct theory of George Kelly, 1959) and in humanistic psychology (e.g., Carl Rogers's notions concerning learning, Rogers, 1969). Without labouring the point, I believe people construct their own worlds. New constructions, new understandings and ways of seeing things, are based on existing constructions and ways of seeing things. I do not see how a person's understanding can significantly develop without involving their existing conceptions, however crude and 'wrong' these are. Also I see significant learning as involving a degree of disorientation and personal threat, and requiring personal autonomy and responsibility from the learner. I am bothering to make these points here because some strategies for helping students to develop as learners are explicitly, or implicitly, based on behavioural models (usually rooted in animal learning therory); on training models (usually rooted in motor skill acquisition theory); or even on models of memory (rooted in the study of the acquisition of unrelated words). This is not merely an academic and esoteric point. It has direct implications for the practical steps one takes when working with students, and I should like to elaborate on these implications.

Taking a student-centred approach

I have been trying for a student-centred approach of some sort ever since the first didactic study skill courses I ran were a disaster. Students start off not as complete blanks, as *tabula rasa,* but with habitual ways of going about reading, writing and discussion, and they develop from and change these ways slowly and with difficulty. They do not adopt entire new approaches wholesale. Conceptions of what learning and studying involve are usually deep-rooted, often based in powerful experiences from school. It is these conceptions which form the framework for the way techniques are adopted and employed. Unless existing habits and conceptions are taken into account, little of significance will occur.

Also the students themselves are in the best position to judge the appropriateness and value of new techniques. Whether a technique suits an individual, whether it meets the demands of the learning tasks, and whether it can be used appropriately given the present level of understanding of learning and level of intellectual development of the individual can only be decided by the individual himself. Our job is to help the individual make the decision.

Giving responsibility to the student

Improvements in studying do not take place only during study skills courses and at no other time. They take place at any and all times during studying and when expert advice is not available. Developing as a learner is a continuous process, and unless the student takes responsibility for this process — for becoming aware of how he is learning and noticing what works and what does not — then change will be impeded. Instead of making students dependent on expert advice and evaluation, self-evaluation and self-awareness should be encouraged. Only when students can see for themselves what the advantages and disadvantages of different ways of going about a study task are is development likely.

There is a tendency to carefully explain to students exactly what is good and bad about some notes or an essay, when in fact they are perfectly capable of judging for themselves. Students are often surprised when they realize they already have plenty of criteria available to them to judge essays, and even more surprised when they discover that their criteria are very similar to their tutor's. In the past they have simply not been in the habit of applying these criteria to themselves, but have left all judgements to teachers. Helping students to judge their studying for themselves is a crucial aspect of helping them to develop as learners.

This emphasis on personal responsibility is based in Carl Rogers's 'principles of learning':

> Learning is facilitated when the student participates responsibly in the learning process. When he chooses his own direction, helps to discover his own learning resources, formulates his own problems, decides his own course of action, lives with the consequences of each of these choices, then significant learning is maximised.

> Independence, creativity and self reliance are all faciliated when self-criticism and self-evaluation are basic . . .
>
> (Rogers, 1969, pp. 162–163)

Making change safe

Studying, and especially assessment, can be very threatening to students. Flexible and effective ways of studying can involve risks. Fransson (1977) has demonstrated experimentally that students who were made highly anxious by a test approached their study in a 'surface processing' way and made ineffective, reproductive attempts to answer the test questions. He concluded: 'If deep level processing is valued, every effort must be made to avoid threatening conditions . . .' This is obviously not a new discovery. Dewey (1913) discussed this effect seventy years ago and the role of threat in inhibiting meaningful learning is a central theme in Carl Rogers's 'principles of learning' (1969), including his fifth principle: 'When threat to the self is low, experience can be perceived in differential fashion, and learning can proceed.' Similarly, analysis of the motivation of students to study suggests that limited, inflexible and surface processing approaches to learning are common among students motivated by a fear of failure (Entwistle and Wilson, 1977; Biggs, 1976).

Under threat we sometimes regress to cruder ways of seeing things which we have employed at an earlier stage in our understanding. Perry (1977) has observed that: '. . . a student, as he loses confidence in himself, tends paradoxically to fall back on less and less productive methods of learning' (p. 123). Similarly, Perry (1970) has described how students revert to earlier stages in their intellectual development when their ideas are under threat. It has always seemed to me that it is exactly those students who are most in need of a more flexible approach to their learning and who feel least secure in the efficiency of their existing approaches who are most deeply entrenched and least likely to change.

Any attempt to help students to develop must provide a safe context for students to examine their existing methods and try out new methods without personal risk. Evaluating students' study methods or their outcomes can obstruct their development.

Emphasizing purpose, rather than technique

This is simply what I argued for above. The emphasis should always be on what study methods are *for* rather than merely on the steps to take to use them. What they are *for* involves the student's overall orientation, conception of learning and stage of intellectual development, and these influence the perceived demands of learning tasks. Techniques should be seen as ways of meeting these demands.

Emphasizing reconceptualization of study tasks

As I argued above, the most important changes which take place as students develop are changes in the way learning is conceptualized and in the epistemological stance taken. Working within a student's existing stage of development allows a certain limited scope for greater efficiency, but often only a broad reconceptualization of what a study task is about will provide scope for significant development. There is little point in teaching a student to go about essay writing in a thoroughly organized and efficient manner if, overall, the student takes a surface approach from an absolutist intention to reproduce the 'right' answer.

Emphasizing students' awareness

I have argued that students become more aware about learning in various ways. They become able to reflect on it, and to recognize and distinguish between various different demands made on them by learning tasks. Above everything else, it is the encouragement of students' active reflection about their studying which is the cornerstone to their development. Simply adopting a new technique will be to little avail if it is not accompanied by the student actively thinking about what he is trying to do with it when it is applied. Sophisticated and inept learners may be almost indistinguishable in terms of their observable study habits. Neither may appear organized. Their notes may look equally haphazard,their essay plans entirely missing. But the sophisticated student will be able to explain the process and purpose underlying his apparently hopeless study methods, while the inept student will be able to say practically nothing about his.

Awareness and reflection are not merely symptoms of developments in learners, they bring about the developments. It is through engaging students in reflecting upon the process and outcomes of their studying that progress is made. Passively following advice results in little such reflection, and so little improvement.

CHAPTER 7

Why use structured group exercises?

The beliefs I expressed in Chapter 5 concerning how people develop as learners can lead to a variety of activities which can be helpful to students. They can be embodied in certain forms of one-to-one study counselling and packaged or distance-learning materials, and they can also be embodied in unstructured group sessions. In certain circumstances I think all these alternatives can be useful, but I would like to explain briefly why I have not proposed them here.

One-to-one study counselling can be extremely effective. As well as being the chosen mode of operation of William Perry at Harvard, to whom I have referred several times, there are two somewhat different models of such help in Britain. Both Wankowski (1979) and Main (1980) have developed and described useful ways of counselling students which embody at least some of the above beliefs. However, such counselling makes enormous demands on the counsellor's facilitative skills if the student is not to be overwhelmed and intimidated by expertise. It is also extremely time consuming. I have found it can take me an hour or so simply to understand enough about the way a student is studying to be able to start working on helping the student to change. And regular counselling meetings between a student's attempts to change everyday habits may be necessary if counselling is not to be seen by the students as an interesting one-off experience unconnected with the everyday activities of studying.

Written materials can also be produced to embody these beliefs. However, examining students' learning habits in a way relevant to their studies involves actual learning and materials would have to include, or be written around, learning materials which are either part of the student's current course, or which are similar in content and the demands they make on the student. A 'learning to learn' manual could be written around a set book for a course, for example, and including reading, note-taking and writing tasks based on the set book. The effort involved in writing such a manual, however, would probably be practical only if the potential audience for the particular course justified it. If student numbers are not large, then methods are needed which are more flexible to the specific demands of courses and students. Inter-active group exercises are both flexible and economical of teachers' time.

To bring about student-centred self-directed learning, it is conventional to use unstructured groups and open, undirected discussion. However, this sort of group many people find very difficult to handle. For the tutor the lack of control may not be felt to be either desirable or possible to achieve given conventional expectations of students for the guidance and control of the tutor. For the students the lack of direction, unclear focus and the characteristically slow early progress of such groups may make them seem a poor investment of time. In addition the dynamics of such groups can lead to discomfort and pressure which the participants might be unwilling to tolerate for the sake of hoping to learn about their studying. Drop-out may be very high, and few tutors feel confident of handling the demanding task of group facilitator. Despite these problems, several professional student counsellors have reported to me the power of unstructured, and even leaderless, groups, once a stable group of students committed to regular meetings has formed.

The form of the structured group exercises which this book proposes overcomes many of these problems. The structure was not developed specifically for this purpose, but as an alternative to conventional tutorials. The structure involves participants starting with their own experience and ideas and progressively opening up and widening these by comparison and contrast with those of the rest of the group. It requires students to work alone, then in pairs, then in small groups of four or six, and finally in a plenary session involving the whole group and chaired by the tutor. This structure was developed by Andrew Northedge (Northedge, 1975) and is widely used as a group discussion technique for all sorts of purposes. It has several advantages: for group dynamics and the way students are able to participate actively in dis-cussion; for the tutor and the way it reduces the demand for either facilitative skills or expertise in study methods; and for the way new ideas and ways of conceptualizing learning can be introduced while still based solidly both in students' own conceptions and experiences and in the particular learning context in which they are working.

The structure involves, in its simplest form, working through four stages.

Working alone

If the discussion is to be rooted in individual student's experiences of relevant learning tasks rather than in generalizations, then it should start with some attempt at accessing student's experience. This can be done either by asking students to think back to particular experiences (e.g., 'the last tutorial you had which was particularly dreadful'), by using various cued recall procedures (e.g., using actual notes taken from a recent lecture to help reconstruct the experience of the lecture) or by providing students with a new and immediate experience (e.g., by requiring them to take notes from a short lecture or article and using these notes as a subsequent focus of discussion). Before discussion of such an experience is begun it is extremely helpful to students to give them time to work up some ideas of their own about it. Many students have difficulty contributing to conventional unstructured discussions. In them, by the time they have thought out what they want to say the focus of the discussion has moved on. Its focus is therefore dominated by the quicker thinking and more confident students, and tends therefore to be concerned with topics other than those with which the silent students are concerned. These students become increasingly disengaged from the discussion, coming to believe that their own ideas are irrelevant. If students are given a short while to think about, and perhaps write down, a couple of things which concern them about the topic this can give them a clearer idea of what they have to say, and a record of it. This can give them more confidence when they come to contribute to later discussion.

The emphasis I have put here on confidence is important. Inexperienced students tend to have very few ideas about how they study, little language to express these ideas, and little confidence in them. In fact it is crucial to define the initial task at this stage in a way that engages students and makes them feel they have *some* ideas about it, and that their ideas are not hopelessly inadequate. Asking a few straightforward questions and suggesting a few straightforward answers about the topic of the exercise can help. For example, instead of simply asking students to look at their notes and to think about them, you might ask: 'Are there parts you feel are very adequate and full enough to make sense of and be useful afterwards, while other parts are too sketchy and unclear to be useful? Why is this? How come you wrote such a sketchy bit of notes? Perhaps you didn't understand something, perhaps you just decided it wasn't important, or perhaps you were writing down so much you got behind. Which parts of your notes are you happy with, and which are you unhappy with, and *why?* Spend five minutes on your own before we go on to discuss note taking.'

It is also possible right at the start, to focus on the *purpose* of some learning activity students have engaged in. For example, it is perfectly feasible simply to ask: 'Why did you take these notes at all? What were you hoping they would do for you?' – and suggest a couple of possible reasons. But questions about *purpose* are harder for students to answer – purpose may never have been considered or is taken for granted – and you may need to give more help and more time, and clear and engaging instructions for students to have anything to say after they have worked alone.

Working in pairs

There are a number of good reasons for asking students to work in pairs rather than to move straight into an open group discussion.

First, it is very much easier to speak in a pair than in a group – in fact it is almost impossible *not* to speak. When ideas are at a very early stage of development the tolerance for ambiguity of meaning and safety from public ridicule (or even being seen to be in a minority) make the exploration and cautious negotiation that is necessary much more likely. Dominant students tend to dominate less, and shyer students can practise and develop their ideas to a point where they are confident enough to try them out in a larger group at the next stage.

Second, it helps to highlight the important aspects of a student's particular way of studying to compare and contrast it with just one other person in some detail. Too much variation at this stage can confuse and obscure differences and lead to a hurried and superficial analysis before ideas have been worked out clearly.

Third, because about half the people in the room will be talking simultaneously at this stage, there is a busy atmosphere and buzz of discussion. This helps make each individual pair anonymous and able to talk without worrying about being overheard. This atmosphere can be enormously facilitative compared with the strained quiet atmosphere common at the start of large group discussions. It encourages participants to get stuck in quickly and confidently.

It can help to give a clear task orientation at this stage to focus pairs' discussion. An easy way to do this is to ask each pair to sort something out between them so that they are agreed on something to take with them to the next stage of the discussion. It can be embarrassing to arrive at the next stage, in groups of four or six, and not have anything to contribute, and so pairs tend to take responsibility for working to make sure they *have* got something to contribute. The absence of a tutor in these discussions encourages this personal responsibility. A task orientation might take the form: 'Discuss the reasons you have found for parts of your notes being more or less useful to you. Are your reasons similar? Agree on the *three most important* reasons and take these three with you to the next stage where you will join another pair who will have their own reasons.'

Working in fours

Once groups become larger than about six they start functioning in rather different ways and progressively become less and less suitable contexts for the personal construction of meaning; for the development of ideas. Instead they become mere platforms for the articulation of the most well worked out and static ideas by the most confident, while most contribute little or nothing. The ideal seems to be to increase the size of the groups, from pairs, sufficiently to introduce a variety of new ideas and new reactions to existing ideas while at the same time maintaining individual's contributions and keeping the whole business relatively safe and unthreatening.

Individuals will have worked out ideas in their pairs, and have some support from their partner to offer and discuss these ideas. Ideas cannot be 'outnumbered' in a group of two pairs and so it is much easier to raise half formed or idiosyncratic ideas which might otherwise be suppressed or ridiculed. The most constructive work gets done at this stage and about half the total time for the exercise should normally be devoted to it.

Again it can be useful to give a group orienting task to help focus discussion. Instructions can be formulated which not only help the discussion, but greatly ease the next, and final, stage as well. For example: 'Between the two pairs in your group you now have six reasons considered most important for why some parts of notes are more useful than others. Discuss these and see if they are similar or overlap. Which of them are most important? Between you agree on just *three* which you would like to contribute to the whole group during the plenary. You may want to modify or combine your reasons to produce your three.'

It can help to ask each group to nominate a 'chairman' to note down the points that are agreed and to act as *rapporteur* during the final plenary.

The progressive opening up to a number of alternative viewpoints, ways of studying and conceptions of learning exposes students to alternatives gradually, in ways expressed in students' rather than experts' language. This is much less threatening than being confronted with an expert conception 'from cold'. Because there has been an opportunity to develop and articulate personal conceptions first, students already have available to them a way of approaching and making sense of these alternatives. This is important when it comes to pooling points in the plenary, as the overall product of the whole group may go far beyond the content of discussions of an individual pair, and yet the product will have considerable validity for the pair because they contributed towards it.

Plenary

This is really a 'reporting back' stage. Its function is to display the similarities and differences between students, and the sheer range of ideas, in public. The development of ideas within individuals may be over by this stage, though seeing others' ideas may encourage some reconceptualization. Its function is to provide a goal for the earlier discussions and legitimacy to their products; to bring to the attention of groups, areas and issues which they did not themselves discuss; to give students an opportunity to ask questions; and to facilitate the development of the students *as a group*.

The plenary may need fairly careful handling if the products of the students' work and discussion are not to be discounted and discredited. It is all too easy to give the impression of saying 'Well all you have said is very interesting, and not bad for beginners, but let me explain it properly for you and correct your misconceptions'. Some tutors have even told me that they use the entire structure simply as a 'softening-up exercise' before they come in with a lecture on 'how to take notes' or whatever the topic is! The product of plenaries can, despite being based only on students' experiences, be very similar to conclusions reached by *How to Study* books, but even when this is not the case it is vital not to cut the ground from under students' feet. All they have to rely on as they develop as learners is their own understanding of what is demanded of them and their judgement about how to meet these demands. If they mistrust their own judgement they will not use it. If plenaries are used to demonstrate to students how poor they are at learning, the whole point of the exercise is lost.

It can be useful to elaborate on students' conclusions, to offer more coherent and articulate ways of expressing the same ideas, provided this is not seen to devalue the students' efforts. It can also be useful to question students in order to get them to clarify their own ideas. A good way to pool the outcome of discussions in fours is to ask each group of four in turn to offer one point or issue. These can be written on a blackboard for display and as a record, once both you and other groups of four are happy about the meaning of the point. What is written on the blackboard can be seen by students to have been acted upon by their colleagues. This makes ideas appear real and credible, rather than merely idealistic, as is often the case with advice, and so more feasible to adopt.

So far I have concentrated on the advantages of this structure for students. Some of my objections to other ways of helping students were more concerned with disadvantages to the 'counsellor' or group leader. What advantages do structured exercises like this offer to the person running such exercises?

The aspect which feedback from teachers emphasizes most is that very few demands are made. There is no demand for great expertise in study techniques, knowledge of literature on student learning or diagnosis of study problems. Common sense and personal experience of studying seem quite sufficient. Students seem to appreciate the person running the exercise revealing strengths and weaknesses of their own studying more than an expert analysis.

There is also very little demand for group facilitative skills. Reading out clear and engaging instructions at the right time does not take much skill. Compared with running a tutorial it is extremely relaxing. I very often even leave the room in order to stop myself interfering or joining groups! Not until the plenary stage is much demand made for sensitivity and non-directive questioning skills.

A consequence of the 'non-expert' role adopted is that the person running the exercise can develop quite a different sort of relationship with students than is customary, in which both parties are jointly trying to understand what is going on in particular learning activities. This helps to transfer responsibility to students for the progress they make.

One of the 'unexpected' outcomes of these exercises, which seems enormously beneficial, is that teachers can discover some of the consequences of their teaching and curricula and how they affect the way students study. If students are being given advice on how to study this does not happen. But if a student-centred exercise is used, teachers can discover that, for example, their students are spending a disproportionate amount of time on an activity not considered important by the teacher. Not all learning problems are the students' fault, and student-centred exercises can be dramatically effective in isolating other causes of ineffective learning. I should like to give a couple of examples here to illustrate this.

I was asked to come in to a language department at a university on one occasion, in order to improve the way their students learnt, which was considered by the lecturers to be inept. One of the students' ineptitudes was considered to be that they read extremely slowly, and I was asked to train them in speed reading techniques. Instead I asked the lecturers to select an example of the sort of reading material they felt students should be reading more of, and in an exercise asked both lecturers and students to start reading the particular book chosen. After a while I simply stopped everyone and asked them to describe to each other what they had been doing and why. Students eventually formed groups of four and then reported their conclusions, and the four lecturers did the same. It emerged that the students had been reading extremely carefully. The book was a parallel text of a classic novel in the particular language, with English on one page and the language on the other. Students had been trying to identify the author's characteristic style and a wide variety of devices of literature: irony, pathos and so on. They had been trying to memorize vocabulary they did not know, and work out grammatical forms with which they were unfamiliar. They were, without exception, reading extremely slowly. In contrast the lecturers had devoured half a chapter in the same time. It quickly emerged that the students had gained completely the wrong impression of what sort of task they had been set. The lecturers explained that they wanted students to get plenty of practice at reading the language, and had chosen the particular novel for its academic respectability, though motorbike magazines or thrillers would have done just as well. Their main concern was for sheer quantity of reading. The students had assumed that universities were concerned with more esoteric matters and were going about their reading for entirely different reasons. There was no study skill problem – only a problem of understanding the demands of a study task, and this was cleared up by making those demands more explicit.

As a second example I have chosen a situation where the diagnosed problem was identical, but the cause quite different. Again a university department in this case a Psychology department, was concerned about the study skills of its first-year students. In particular they seemed not to be reading enough. The scale of this problem quickly became apparent when, in an exercise on how students actually spent their time before and after the course started, it emerged that students had actually been reading *more* psychology *before* the course started! But the cause was not far away. Three-quarters of all their time outside class contact hours was spent writing up laboratory reports! This turned out to be because laboratory reports were marked severely and the students were worried about not passing the first year. In fact there was a pass-fail entry into the second year and a student would have had to commit murder to fail, but the students did not know this. Their lack of reading was a direct consequence of a fear of failure and their perceived demands of the assessment system. Again, apparent poor study skill was caused by teachers.

If teaching students to learn is undertaken by specialist counsellors or study skill experts — because it is seen as a very demanding teaching task — then these sorts of outcomes seldom get back to teachers and the root of the learning problem is never tackled. Only if an approach is adopted which is so easy that teachers can use it in the context of their own departments, even in their own classrooms, is it likely that they will be tackled. In every exercise I have ever run issues have arisen which were to do with *constraints* on students' learning over which the students had no control. To approach teaching students to learn in a way which does not bring out these issues is to ignore half the problem. Either giving advice, or using specialist agencies to undertake the task, is to ignore half the problem.

This brings me to the final point that I should like to make in this book: that you can bring a horse to water, but you cannot make him drink. Occasions will inevitably arise, if you use this approach, where your own and your students' goals in education become clarified publicly, and they are found to be profoundly different: where what you want your students to be doing is different from what they are doing and what they say they want to be doing. I have had students tell me after a series of exercises that they could now see the way they *could* go about studying on their course, but that they were not going to because it was not necessary to do so in order to pass their examinations. All this approach can hope to do is to help students to be in a position where they can see and understand the learning options open to them, and where their awareness makes them free to make their own decisions as to what to do. It may take fundamental changes in the whole educational context within which students study for them to choose to study in the way you would like them to.

Selected further reading

HILLS, P. J. (Ed.) (1979) *Study Courses and Counselling*, Society for Research into Higher Education. This is a collection of articles written by those responsible for having developed a variety of different practical approaches to improving students' study methods in Britain. It is a somewhat partial selection, and a good deal of material has been published elsewhere, but it contains useful introductions to the use of 'contracts' with students (Goldman), to individual study counselling (Wankowski), and descriptions of several study skills courses.

British Journal of Guidance and Counselling, (1979) Vol. 7, No 1, January. This issue, of a journal which often contains useful articles on counselling students about study problems, examination anxiety, and so on, is largely devoted to different approaches to developing study methods. It contains several of the same authors as the Hills collection of articles (see above) and an article by Helweg-Larsen concerning training methods developed by Tony Buzan's Learning Methods Group to introduce patterned, or 'organic' note-taking techniques.

MAIN, ALEX (1980) *Encouraging Effective Learning*, Scottish Academic Press, Edinburgh. This is a handbook for teachers who do not want simply to give study skills advice but do not have any counselling skills. Its analysis of what learning consists of is very conventional and is centred around relatively mechanical study skills, though it avoids the inanities of *How to Study* manuals. It reviews contemporary research into student learning but makes no use of this in its fundamentally pragmatic one-to-one teaching methods. It has a comprehensive guide to where to find study skills advice on different topics. Most useful in its detailed examples of how individual students can be dealt with.

ENTWISTLE, NOEL and HOUNSELL, DAI (1975) *How Students Learn,* Readings in Higher Education, 1, University of Lancaster.
A well-selected collection of articles reflecting the range of perspectives that exist on how students learn. At one end of the spectrum are the behaviourists and animal learning theorists (e.g., Skinner) applying formal psychological theories. In the middle, cognitive psychologists and information processing theorists. And at the other extreme, are humanistic psychologists (e.g., Rogers and Maslow). Articles by Marton and by Perry are particularly recommended. These articles are not directly concerned with applications of their perspectives to practical problems of student learning, but the editors give a useful overview of implications for teaching.

References

BEATY, L. (1978) 'The student study contract', Lancaster 4th International Conference on Higher Education.

BECKER, M.S., GREER, B and HUGHES, E.C. (1968) *Making the Grade: the Academic Side of College Life,* New York, Wiley.

BIGGS, J.B. (1976) 'Dimensions of study behaviour: another look at A.T.I.' *British Journal of Educational Psychology,* Vol. 46, 68—80.

BOOK, W.F. (1925) *The Psychology of Skill,* New York, Gregg.

BRITTON, J., BURGESS, T., MARTIN, N., McLEOD, A. and ROSEN, H. (1975) *The Development of Writing Abilities.* London: Methuen/Schools Council.

BUZAN, T. (1973) *Use Your Head,* BBC.

COLAIZZI, P.F. (1973) 'Reflection and Research in Psychology: A phenomenological study of learning', Dubuque: Kendall/Hunt.

CRAWFORD, C.C. (1925) 'The correlation between lecture notes and quiz papers', *Journal of Educational Research,* Vol. 12, 379—386.

DAHLGREN, L.O. (1979a) 'Understanding students' understanding — some qualitative aspects of the process and outcome of teaching and learning at University level', Reports from the Institute of Education, University of Göteborg, No. 80, January 1979.

DAHLGREN, L.O. (1979b) 'Children's conception of price as a function of questions asked', Reports from the Institute of Education, University of Göteborg, No. 81, March 1979.

DEWEY, J. (1913) *Interest and Effort in Education,* Boston, Houghton Mifflin.

EBBINGHAUS, M. (1885) *Uber das Gedachtmis,* Leipzig, Dunker and Humbolt.

EDFELDT, A.E. (1976) 'A det meningsfullt med studieteknisk traning?' ('Is there a meaningful study-skill training?') *Forskning om utbildring,* Vol. 3, 15—24.

EISNER, S. and ROHDE. (1959) 'Note-taking during or after the lecture', *Journal of Educational Psychology,* Vol. 50, 301—304.

ENTWISTLE, N. (1977) 'Strategies of learning and studying: recent research findings' *British Journal of Educational Studies.*

ENTWISTLE, N. and HOUNSELL, D. (eds) (1975) *How Students Learn. Readings in Higher Education, 1,* Institute for Research and Development in Post Compulsory Education, University of Lancaster.

ENTWISTLE, N. and WILSON, J. (1977) *Degrees of Excellence: The Academic Achievement Game,* London, Hodder and Stoughton.

FARRELL, J.F. (1977) 'Study habits and academic achievements: Part 1 — a review of the field', *Bulletin of Educational Research,* Vol. 13, 25–32.

FRANSSON, A. (1977) 'On qualitative differences in learning: IV — Effects of intrinsic motivation and extrinsic test anxiety on process and outcome', *British Journal of Educational Psychology,* Vol. 47, 244–257.

FREEMAN, R. (1972) *How to Study Effectively,* National Extension College.

GADZELLA, B.M., GOLDSTON, J.T. and ZIMMERMAN, M.L. (1977) 'Effectiveness of exposure to study techniques on college students' perceptions', *Journal of Educational Psychology,* Vol. 71, 26–30.

GIBBS, G. (1977) *Learning to Study — A Guide to Running Group Sessions.* Institute of Educational Technology, The Open University.

GIBBS, G., MORGAN, A. and TAYLOR, L. (1980) 'Understanding Why Students Don't Learn', *Study Methods Group Report No. 5.* Institute of Educational Technology, The Open University.

GOLDMAN, G. (1979) 'A contract for academic improvement', in P.J. HILLS (ed.) *Study Courses and Counselling,* Society for Research into Higher Education.

GOLDMAN, R.D. (1972) 'Effects of logical versus a mnemonic learning strategy on performance in two undergraduate psychology classes', *Journal of Educational Psychology,* Vol. 63, 347–352.

HARTLEY, J. and CAMERON, A. (1967) 'Some observations on the efficiency of lecturing', *Educational Review,* Vol. 20, 30–37.

HARTLEY, J. and TRUEMAN (1978) 'Note-taking in lectures: A longitudinal study', *Bulletin of the British Psychology Society,* Vol. 31, 37–39.

HILLS, P.J. (ed.) (1979) 'Study courses and counselling problems and possibilities', *Research into Higher Education Monographs,* Society for Research into Higher Education, University of Surrey.

HOWE, M.J.A. (1977) 'Learning and the acquisition of knowledge by students: some experimental investigations', in M.J.A. HOWE, (ed.) *Adult Learning: Psychological Research and Applications,* London, Wiley.

HOWE, M. and GODFREY, J. (1978) *Student Note Taking as an Aid to Learning.* Exeter University Teaching Services, Exeter University.

KAGAN, N. (1975) 'Influencing human interaction – 11 years with IPR', *Canadian Counsellor,* Vol. 9, 74–97.

KELLY, G. (1959) *The Psychology of Personal Constructs,* New York, Norton.

LAURILLARD, D. (1979) 'Research methods in student learning'. EARDHE Congress, Klagenfort

McCLENDON, P. (1978) 'An experimental study of the relationships between the note-taking practices and listening comprehension of college freshmen during expository lectures', *Speech Monographs,* Vol. 25, 222–228.

MACMANAWAY, L.A. (1968) 'Using lecture scripts', *Universities Quarterly,* Vol. 22, 327–336.

MADDOX, H. (1963) *How to Study,* Pan Books.

MAIN, A. (1977) 'Using your time', 2nd videotape in series: *Study Patterns* Glasgow, Centre for Educational Practice, Strathclyde University.

MAIN, A. (1980) *Encouraging Effective Learning,* Scottish Academic Press, Edinburgh.

MARTON, F. (1975) 'What does it take to learn?' in ENTWISTLE and HOUNSELL (Eds), *How Students Learn.*

MARTON, F. and SÄLJÖ, R. (1976a) 'On qualitative differences in learning: I – Outcome and process', *British Journal of Educational Psychology,* Vol. 46, 4–11.

MATHIAS, H. (1978) 'Science students' approaches to learning', Lancaster 4th International Conference on Higher Education.

MILLER, C.M.L. and PARLETT, M.R. (1974) *Up to the Mark: a Study of the Examination Game,* Society for Research into Higher Education, London.

NORTHEDGE, A. (1975) 'Learning through discussion in the Open University', *Teaching at a Distance,* No. 2, Open University.

Open University, (1979) *Preparing to Study.* Open University Press.

PARLETT, M., SIMONS, H., SIMONDS, R. and NEWTON, E. (1976) *Learning from Learners,* Nuffield Foundation.

PERRY, W.G. (1959). 'Students use and misuse of reading skills', *Harvard Educational Review,* Vol. 29, No. 3, 193–200.

PERRY, W.G. (1970) *Forms of Intellectual and Ethical Development in the College Years: A Scheme.* New York, Holt, Rinehart and Winston.

PERRY, W.G. (1977) 'Studying and the student', *Higher Education Bulletin,* Vol. 5, No. 2.

PETERS, D.L. (1972) 'Effects of note-taking and rate of presentation on short-term objective test performance', *Journal of Educational Psychology,* Vol. 63, 276–280.

RAMSDEN, P. (1979) 'Student learning in context — the relationship between student learning and perceptions of the academic environment', *Higher Education, 8.*

REID, F. (1977) 'A preliminary evaluation of the advanced learning and reading course, in the development and evaluation of study skills courses for students in higher education', Occasional Paper 4. Standing Conference on Educational Development Services in Polytechnics.

ROGERS, C. (1969). *Freedom to Learn.* Columbus, Ohio, Merrill.

SÄLJÖ R. (1978) 'Learning about learning', Lancaster 4th International Conference on Higher Education.

SÄLJÖ, R. (1979a) 'Learning in the learner's perspective I — some commonsense conceptions' , *Reports from the Institute of Education,* University of Göteborg, No. 76.

SÄLJÖ, R. (1979b) 'Learning in the learner's perspective II — differences in awareness', *Reports from the Institute of Education,* University of Göteborg, No. 77.

SÄLJÖ, R. (1979c) 'Learning in the learner's perspective IV — considering one's own strategy', *Reports from the Institute of Education,* University of Göteborg, No. 79.

SNYDER, B. (1971) *The hidden curriculum,* MIT.

SVENSSON, L. (1976) 'Study skill and learning, *Göteborg Studies in Educational Sciences, 19,* Acta Universitatis Gothoburgensis, Ph.D. Thesis.

SVENSSON, L. (1977) 'On qualitative differences in learning: III — Study skill and learning', *British Journal of Educational Psychology,* Vol. 47, 223–243.

TYLER, R.W. (1933) 'The permanence of learning', *Journal of Higher Education,* Vol. 4.

WANKOWSKI, J. (1979) 'Educational counselling and learning-through-teaching', *British Journal of Guidance and Counselling,* Vol. 7, No. 1. 72–79.

WITKIN, M.A., MOORE, C.A., GOODENOUGH, D.R. and COX, P.W. (1977) 'Field-dependent and independent cognitive styles and their educational implications', *Review of Educational Research,* Vol. 47, No. 1, 1.

Index

109

seminars, 6, 46
serialist (holist) approach, 72, 78–79
'skimming' of books, 24
Snyder, B., 80
social pressure, on students, 15, 52
structured discussion technique, 45, 93
student-centred approach, 51, 57, 88
students:
  experience of studying, 3, 5, 13–14, 45–6, 94
  attitude to exercises, 4
  non-passive role of, 7
  laziness of, 11
  ability to organize, 15–17
  social pressures on, 15, 52
  note-taking by, 19–20
  responsibility taken by, 39, 88–9, 98
  habits hard to change, 49–50, 66–7, 86
  unable to take advice, 68–9
  choice of study habits, 72–5
  conception of learning, 81–3
  awareness of, 90–1
'Students' use and mis-use of reading skills (Perry), 26 fn, 26–33
study contract, *see* contracts
study groups:
  composition and size, 3–5
  non-passive role of students in, 7
  exercises for, 10–44 *passim*
  reasons for using structured exercises, 92–100
study habits inventories, 47, 60
'Study Skill and Learning', 75
surface approach, 76, 78, 83, 89, 90
Surrey, University of, survey, 76
Svensson, L., 76, 78–9
syllabus-bound behaviour, 73

'Taking notes', 18–23, 46, 48–9, 50, 58, 93–4
  studies about, 59, 67
  training in, 70
teachers (tutors):
  role of, in study group, 4–5
  time required for preparation, 7–9, 93
  experience of exercises, 8
  design their own exercises, 9, 10, 45–55 *passim*
  quality of, 11
  advice given by, 16, 68–9
  feedback to students, 38–73
  poor communication with students, 99–100
threat-free study groups, 5, 24, 89–90, 96–7
time for study:
  organization of, 5, 15–16
  commitment to, 80
timetabling, of study improvement courses, 52
timing, of exercises, 48
training, in study habits, 69–70
training models, 87
Trueman, M., *see* Hartley, J.
tutorials, 6
  video-recordings of, 46
  personal accounts of, 47
  method of organizing, 57
tutors, *see* teachers
Tyler, R.W., 62

understanding:
  of subject matter, 14
  of nature of learning, 53
  learning as, 80–2
  of learning options, 100
Use Your Head (BBC), 61
using books, *see* 'Reading – using books'

video-recordings, of tutorials, 46

Wankowski, J., 92

110